MILK & HONEY

CAMBRIA JOY

HARVEST HOUSE PUBLISHERS
EUGENE, OREGON

 CONTENTS

NEW TESTAMENT

As we begin our journey of
nourishment in the garden
and make our way through
THE LAND OF MILK & HONEY,
may we have an appetite for
the bread and the cup when
Jesus holds it out to us.
May we gladly receive life
that completely quenches our
thirst yet forever makes us
HUNGRY FOR MORE OF HIM.

TASTE & SEE

Taste and see that the LORD is good.
Oh, the joys of those who take refuge in him!

PSALM 34:8 NLT

Taste and see? Exactly. First we'll taste, and then maybe we'll see. Our skepticism reaches beyond our plates and to our souls. It's hard to trust anything we see today. Everything seems to have a perfect filter or a catch. We're not quick to agree that something is good or even real until we experience it ourselves. Whether that means taking a bite or taking off a mask—we want to see how things really are, not just how they appear to be. We safeguard ourselves, from our lips to our hearts, so our expectations don't collide with reality; we'd rather have them coincide. What happens when the shiny veneer comes off and we're left with disappointment? Our walls go up. We *knew* it. What seemed too good to be true was. But you know what's even more disappointing than unmet expectations? Never having a bite at all.

This devotional is an invitation to taste and see that God is good. With God, there is no facade. God doesn't tell us he's good and demand we believe it. He invites us to bring our skepticism and our spoons and to taste with our own lips rather than hear about his love from someone else or make assumptions about him. He wants us to discover his goodness is real because our taste buds reveal it's true: He is sweeter than honey straight from the comb.

We're going to taste test our way through Scripture as we savor a verse from each book of the Bible—Genesis to Revelation. Together, we'll dig in for ourselves to what the psalmist wrote: "Oh, taste and see that the LORD is good!" (Psalm 34:8). Why? Because God wired us for nourishment.

Our stomachs remind us of our physical need every few hours. Our souls remind us of our spiritual need constantly. We feel the ache in the marrow of our bones for something more out of life. More than money. More than stuff we buy with that money. More than a "perfect" reflection in the mirror. Is the solution just that—do we only need a little more? But we're dry and hungry still. We feel the emptiness and the dissatisfaction still. Jesus knew we would feel this way: "Everyone who drinks of this water will be thirsty again, but whoever drinks of the water that I will give him will never be thirsty again" (John 4:13-14). Satisfaction is here, now.

There's a reason Jesus often uses food and drink metaphors to offer us a tangible grip on spiritual things: We know, not only in our heads but in our hearts and lives, the reality of things unseen. Spiritual truths are as real as the water we drink and the food we eat.

Why live constantly trying to curb our appetites? Why keep going back to the same well that's proven to leave us thirsty? We don't want to live in spiritual survival mode, barely getting by, when all along, Jesus offers us abundant life. The promise of satisfaction is found in his nail-imprinted hands, proof he gave his life so we could be nourished to life eternally.

From beginning to end, nourishment is woven into Scripture. From the fruit on the trees of Eden to the manna in the middle of the desert, all the way to the Last Supper and looking ahead to the marriage feast of the lamb; it is so clear God wants to satiate the hunger within our souls. He wants to provide for us. He wants to sustain us. More than anything, he wants to overflow our lives so they drip with his abundant goodness, inviting others to taste too. So as we begin our journey of nourishment in the garden and make our way through the land of milk and honey, may we have an appetite for the bread and the cup when Jesus holds it out to us. May we gladly receive life that completely quenches our thirst yet forever makes us hungry for more of him.

I wrote this for myself as much as I wrote this for you because I know it's easy to become undernourished in life and wake up worried, dissatisfied, burdened, discouraged, and insecure. It seems we're always running on empty. At one point, I found myself knowing a lot *about* Jesus but missing *Jesus*. His love forever radiates warmth; I had just wandered away from the fire. It clicked when I realized the greatest commandment isn't to know *about* God but to *love* God with everything we are. The thing is, the more you love someone, the more you *want* to know them. So let's come back to our first love.

We don't want our walk with God to turn into a restrictive diet, because then we dip our toes into religion rather than relationship. Coming to Jesus consistently—not out of obligation but because of a personal invitation to be satisfied in him—nourishes our souls. That's where the life is. As we take in the pure milk of the Word, we'll mature and be prepared to receive greater nourishment that takes us deeper. We become fortified. We move from milk to honey. We walk with Jesus and then learn to run with endurance and strength in the race he's set before us. We enter into the unfolding story of God, and it energizes us and awakens our souls back to life—all because we've come to the table. Pull up a chair; you belong here. My hope is that you'll find "good" only scratches the surface. Come, taste, and see.

OLD TESTAMENT

God's redemptive plan to nourish us back to life with his Son is unearthed in every prophecy, proverb, and picture in the ancient texts before his birth. Let's take our seat at the table; we're invited to taste and see—and to feel the beat of his heart for us—from Genesis to Malachi.

A TASTE OF
ACCEPTANCE

He said, "Who told you that you were naked? Have you eaten of the tree of which I commanded you not to eat?"

GENESIS 3:11

The solution for our broken souls isn't sewn-together fig leaves. It's already hard to face our own vulnerabilities in the mirror; shame can be present even when someone else's presence is not. But another person's eyes can magnify the insecurity we already feel inside. The shadows invite us to abandon our Maker. They deceive us with the idea that his light wants to expose us rather than redeem us. It seems we can feel the same today as we did in Eden. We forget that his light isn't a glaring spotlight but a warm, welcoming glow that draws us in with grace. We won't find wholeness if we try to conceal our brokenness; the paradox is that the only way we can be made whole is to bring our brokenness into the light.

I've been a follower of Jesus for as long as I can remember and have always believed in him, yet I still need constant reminders of my everyday need for him too. I deeply desired to have a rich and dynamic relationship with God, to live my life on purpose and with purpose. I didn't just want to know *about* Jesus; I wanted to *know* Jesus and have him know me in a real, life-changing way. But I didn't realize how much I would have to unlearn about him in order to swim deeper into the waters of my faith; I had to untether myself from a performance-based relationship where I felt like I failed him regularly. Even though I loved him, I struggled to find the motivation to prioritize a daily walk with him because I felt guilty that my most frequent prayers were cries for help rather than daily conversations with my Father. I felt like I was using God, and that made me feel ashamed. I believed I was disappointing him, like the person you never hear from except when they need something from you. I knew in my head that wasn't true, but my heart struggled to embrace a grace-based relationship with him. It was only when I unanchored myself from the lie that God's acceptance was based on me being "good enough" that I was able to swim freely into a vibrant, authentic relationship with him based on his goodness, not mine. And even more than that, he came and searched me out in the shadows. That doesn't mean shame never lurks around; I just choose to listen to the truth that's steeped in grace and step into the light. And that's what set me free. Or rather, *who* set me free.

Shame blinds us because it keeps our eyes on ourselves rather than our Redeemer. Yet in the garden, we catch our first glimpse of the heart of God. He doesn't push us away in shame but pulls us in with love. Think about it: How we respond to people when they wrong us says a lot about who we are. When someone bumps into you, what spills out? Frustration? Grace? Resentment? Kindness? Revenge? *Cleanup on aisle me.*

Yet when Adam and Eve disobeyed God, how did he respond? He didn't yell at them and tell them they were naked. He went to look for them. He didn't withdraw from them or give them the silent treatment. He talked to them. And he didn't stomp toward the bushes in the heat of anger but walked toward them in the cool of the day. The first words out of his mouth weren't "What did you do?" but "Where are you?" Connection is at the heart of God's heart, and we are secure in him because of his love. When you feel safe, there's no reason to hide any part of you, from your skin to the secrets of your soul. Because shame withers in the light of love.

So may we step into the light because shame dissolves in his grace-abounding gaze as he looks at us through eyes of love. The God who formed us from the dust in the garden is the God who stooped down as the rabbi from Nazareth to wash the dust from his disciples' feet. It's in our mess we see his acceptance of us is crystal clear. He doesn't see our failures; he sees his bride. May we hear Jesus say to each of us, *Come as you are.*

A TASTE OF
HELP

*Moses' father-in-law said to him, "What you are
doing is not good. You and the people with you will
certainly wear yourselves out, for the thing is too
heavy for you. You are not able to do it alone."*

EXODUS 18:17-18

We have twenty-four hours in a day, and hopefully, a third of those are spent in dreamland. It's practically a full-time job to do the stuff of everyday life: going to the grocery store, doing your laundry, scrubbing the dishes for the thousandth time, and regularly getting in time on your workout mat—the list goes on. And on. Whatever you're doing, I know one thing is for sure: It's a lot. It seems "busy" is not something we do but someone we've become. And even though we aren't Moses trying to lead millions of people through the wilderness, the timeless truth still stands: We're not meant to carry the load of life alone.

Yes, even Moses hit a wall trying to help God's people. Did God cancel Moses's calling because his servant needed help? Of course not. Yet today we find shame instead of grace when we could use a hand. In this case, Moses didn't carry a physical burden. He carried the emotional weight of others as he listened to them, prayed for them, and guided them to relate better to God and others. This was good work. But just because work is good doesn't mean it's good to do it alone. Perhaps like Moses, you've found that the schedules, deadlines, to-do lists, and appointments are wearing out your soul. Even life-giving work, the kind that helps others and honors God, is too much to do alone. Ever wake up after a full night's sleep and still feel weary in your soul? We don't often realize the pressure we're under until we're broken by it or buried under its weight.

We don't even see Jesus doing work without help. Could he do it alone? Of course. He is the flesh and bone of God himself. Surely nothing is impossible for him. But he modeled a life that was not spent overwhelmed and buried under the demands of people. He regularly retreated from the crowds to be alone with his Father. He shouldered the weight of ministry with his disciples. Jesus knew how to pour out *and* fill up.

There's nothing wrong with having goals or wanting to be productive. Balance needs to be part of our pursuits because it doesn't feel good or please God when we struggle under the weight of a heavy to-do list. If we are worn-out from the moment we open our eyes until we climb back into bed, it's not time to pick up the pace and push through. It's time to realize strength is found not in our ability to get it all done but in letting go of the pressure to do it all. Of course, it's not about neglecting responsibility. But the right response to a heavy load is not to lift it yourself. Just because you can't get it all done, you're not a failure. You're human. God looks at us not only as his people but also as his flock. We're sheep, and in the best way: "We are his people, and the sheep of his pasture" (Psalm 100:3). Guess what sheep don't do? They don't lift heavy things. They don't carry burdens. They don't really do a whole lot of anything except follow their shepherd around. The shepherd protects and guides, and those in his charge simply receive his care because that's all they can really do.

The weight of burnout is heavy, but the burden of Jesus is light. Jethro tells Moses that once he releases the pressure to carry it all himself, his days will be easier, his load lighter, his steps directed by God, and his endurance greater. Even the people will have more peace. Don't believe the lie that the strongest thing you can do is never let go. You know the weight of the world can't be carried with two hands. Remember, our job isn't primarily to carry but to follow. To follow Jesus. Rest is found not in reaching the finish line but in following the shepherd. May we come to Jesus and find that the heaviest thing we carry is the truth that sets us free.

A TASTE OF
REST

Six days shall work be done, but on the seventh day is a
Sabbath of solemn rest, a holy convocation. You shall do no
work. It is a Sabbath to the LORD in all your dwelling places.

LEVITICUS 23:3

I t seems there's not a lot we look forward to more than the
chance to go on vacation. To break away from the cares of this
life and refresh our souls. Just the thought of that makes me
want to exhale. Even the hope of time to recover and restore can
ease our tension temporarily. We can settle for the hope of rest
but not follow through because of life demands or even misplaced
guilt about having a break.

We regularly need to breathe a little deeper and go a little
slower. Not just once a year for seven days but as a regular part of
our weekly rhythm. Sabbath isn't a religious commandment meant
to enslave us but a life-giving invitation meant to refresh us. Does
God not understand we have a never-ending to-do list? A whole
day of rest sounds nice, but there are bills, deadlines, and well, *life*.

Jesus had such a full life, he barely had time to eat some days.
Sound familiar? Take a look: "And he said to them, 'Come away

by yourselves to a desolate place and rest a while.' For many were coming and going, and they had no leisure even to eat" (Mark 6:31). Jesus knew what it was like to have so many demands that he was forced to skip lunch. He's not out of touch with us. He felt the pains of busyness in his soul too. And that's exactly why he repeatedly shows us a life of rest—from God resting on the seventh day of creation to Jesus resting on the Sabbath day. A kind of rest that goes deeper than a deep-tissue massage.

Now, don't get me wrong, a spa day can be a great thing. Esther basically got beauty treatments for a year. I love a good pedicure and an afternoon lounging beneath palm trees while sipping cucumber water. However, our invitation to rest isn't just about going to a resort. So where do we go? I think the place Jesus led his disciples is the same place he invites us to: a desolate place. Yes, a place without inhabitants. In other words, you simply need to be alone. And by "alone," I mean you and God. Rest isn't a location but a posture of the heart. A heart that bows in reverence to be still before God. To get quiet enough to hear his voice.

Work requires us to repeat tasks day after day. The monotony can dull our hearing and make it hard to listen to the still, small voice of God, who desires to freely give us rest when we come to him. The remedy? Just like we roll up our sleeves to get to work, we have to roll up our sleeves when it comes to rest. The challenge before us is to focus our attention on God in a world that's loud. We're pulled in different directions all day, but if we direct our attention to God moment by moment, we'll find that even demanding days can't deafen us to his whispers.

It takes diligence to wake up and slow down, to spend time with the One who gives us true life. We rush through our lives hungry for rest, but all the while Jesus freely hands it out. All we have to do is come to him to receive this soul-satisfying nourishment not bought with wages but given out by God: "Do not work for the food that perishes, but for the food that endures to eternal life, which the Son of Man will give to you" (John 6:27). We get full when we fill up on the words of Jesus. There's no need to hurry through our days full of weariness when he offers us endurance by simply resting in his presence: "Come to me, all who labor and are heavy laden, and I will give you rest" (Matthew 11:28).

Go to him. Streams of quiet waters are found everywhere our Shepherd goes. Jesus promised when we come to *him*—a person, not a place—our souls find rest. I hope you hear the echo of God's heart when he says, "Come away." He wants to do more than relax you. He wants to regenerate you. You'll return beyond refreshed—you'll be made completely new. He's just waiting for you to say yes. May you take his hand today and find your soul refreshed every step of the way.

A TASTE OF
GRATITUDE

We remember the fish we ate in Egypt that cost nothing,
the cucumbers, the melons, the leeks, the onions, and
the garlic. But now our strength is dried up, and
there is nothing at all but this manna to look at.

NUMBERS 11:5-6

God has a will for your life. There's something God made you to do. Or rather, someone he made you to be. All you need to do is give thanks in every single circumstance in your life, no matter what. Simple? Yes. Easy? Not so much. Because that little word "all" sneaks up on us, doesn't it? The Bible says, "Give thanks in all circumstances; for this is the will of God in Christ Jesus for you" (1 Thessalonians 5:18). You know what other little word can sneak up on us? "In." We're told to give thanks "in" all circumstances, not "for" all circumstances. Even when discontentment and impatience flourish around us like weeds, we can still be grateful. It becomes easier to give thanks in all circumstances when we understand that all things work together for our good.

Gratefulness invites us to step back and look at the bigger picture of life with refreshed awe. It seems we regularly need this shift in perspective because we normalize miracles. It's a miracle we're all even alive right now, spinning around on this planet. Shouldn't we freak out over the fact that none of our fingerprints are even remotely the same?

If we lose our sense of wonder, we can wander so far away from gratitude that we fail to express our appreciation for even the smallest things. There is no downside to saying thank you. Thankfulness is not the result of satisfaction; thankfulness is the root of satisfaction.

Contentment isn't something that's found. It's something that's cultivated. Giving thanks enables us to be content. When the Israelites complain on their way to the promised land, they are reminiscing about the days of fish and vegetables during their *enslavement.* Why would anyone want to go back to slavery for some cucumbers and fish? How could they be so ready to abandon their current freedom for the sake of passing pleasure? Their hearts are so void of thankfulness, they even insult the miracle of manna, the food rained down from heaven by God. Their desire for satisfaction is not wrong—it's misplaced.

We desire satisfaction because we've been created by the One who "satisfies the longing soul, and the hungry soul he fills with good things" (Psalm 107:9). Problems arise when our search for satisfaction takes us down a road away from God. Thankfulness to our Father keeps us on the right path, no matter what ground we currently stand on. For years, I looked for satisfaction in the mirror. I thought if I could control what I brought to my lips, my heart would eventually find contentment. But the more I tried to control my body, the more it began to control me. I freely walked right into bondage, thinking freedom was in the perfecting of my own image, rather than finding satisfaction in knowing I am made in the image of the One who created me.

God has freed us from the pressure to gain satisfaction through our own efforts. It takes time to see that as a gift. The more I tried to find fullness outside of God, the emptier I felt. Nothing was ever enough: a lower number on the scale, a different jean size, the praise of people. It took me a long time to realize there's only one promise keeper, and his name isn't "more." It's Jesus.

When we look at Jesus's life, it's shocking because we see the opposite of "more." His body was broken, not perfected. His last possession was not saved in a bank but gambled away. His followers leaving rather than remaining loyal. And still, Jesus alone . . . is everything. The search for satisfaction ends when "more" is overthrown as king and Jesus takes his rightful place on the throne as Lord of our lives. Let's not use our freedom to go back to what we've been delivered from. If we try to satiate our appetite on our own, we'll go around in circles. There's a direct route to satisfaction, and it's the road that ends at the cross.

The only "more" that will fill us is more of him. When we finally taste the honey of the promised land, may we declare we've found nothing sweeter than Jesus alone. We'll find contentment isn't the greener grass our feet stand on but a person alive within our heart. And whether we're in the empty wilderness or a land of abundance, we remember he is our daily bread wherever we are. Because he is on our lips, may "thank you" be too.

A TASTE OF
FULLNESS

*When I have brought them into the land flowing with milk
and honey, which I swore to give to their fathers, and they
have eaten and are full and grown fat, they will turn to other
gods and serve them, and despise me and break my covenant.*

DEUTERONOMY 31:20

Nothing reveals what's going on inside our hearts quite like the passing of time. There's a reason we get antsy if a red light is too long. Stillness makes us stir. We worry if we have to wait too long. The need for patience can make us panic. Outside circumstances have a way of changing the inner landscape of our hearts.

The dry wilderness seems like an ideal landscape to inspire a thirst for God. Yet the Israelites grew frustrated when they had to wait too long for their leader, Moses, on Mount Sinai. They finally threw up their hands toward God and, in an act of exasperation, built another god with their own hands. Their love grew cold as their impatience burned hot. It's interesting that when the apostle Paul talks about love in 1 Corinthians 13, he first describes it as "patient."

The Israelites left behind their first love because of what? Impatience. We typically avoid being acquainted with patience. We'd prefer to rule over time rather than be subject to it. Our perception of time, though, is very different from God's. To us, twenty-four hours is a day, but to God, one day is a thousand years, and at the same time, a thousand years is one day.

So my question is, *Who are we in the middle?* In the in-between, who do we become? Do we allow impatience to bend our view of God? Or do we give the truth time to form within us a proper perspective of him? What if the delay is preparing our hearts to hold the promise? Maybe our hands need to learn to hold tighter to God's good *hand* than the good *land*.

God knows a belly full of milk and honey has the potential to give us a forgetful heart. When we experience the goodness of God in our lives and enjoy the blessings he gives us, do we remember to turn back and thank him, or do we go on our way filled with good but forgetful of the best? If we don't thirst for him in the dry wilderness, how will we remember to drink of him in "a good land—a land with brooks, streams, and deep springs gushing out into the valleys and hills" (Deuteronomy 8:7 NIV)? If we leave God for his gifts, there will be no greater exercise in missing the point. The promised land becomes dangerous territory if we arrive only to be filled with everything but him. Better to walk with him forever and never arrive than to get there only to leave him. Good was designed not to empty us of God but to fill us with remembrance of him. Because maybe the real test isn't the wilderness but the promised land.

The ground is ready. The soil is rich. God has good plans for you. He's preparing in us now what he has for our future, but first the hardness of our hearts must be tilled up in order to receive the goodness. Fear wants us to hurry and make us believe God is slow. Our fear of missing out leads us all over the place as we chase "good enough" rather than wait for the blessings of God's "enough." They look nothing alike. Our substitutions don't last or satisfy.

Let's believe wholeheartedly that God is not slow. He is good, and that means he prepares both the land and the landscape of our hearts. Make friends with patience. Don't listen to fear, because it will only trip you up along the way. Remember, time is nothing more than a tool in the hand of God to chisel the hurry out of our hearts. Remember him. Taste the bread and the cup, and you won't be filled with forgetfulness when you taste the milk and honey. Jesus is our promised land.

A TASTE OF
CERTAINTY

The LORD your God dried up the waters of the Jordan for
you until you passed over, as the LORD your God did to the
Red Sea, which he dried up for us until we passed over.

JOSHUA 4:23

One of the certainties of life is uncertainty. We want to live our lives free from the grip of worry, but how do we do that when the road before us holds so many unknowns? We don't know what we don't know. All we do know is we can't see around the corner, which makes it easy for unfamiliarity to open the door to fear. But what if our solution to worry isn't found in a crystal-clear future but in our rock-solid past? We arrive at the brink of the promised land with the rising waters of the Jordan River before us, and though our eyes see a dead end, our mind resurfaces memories of a wall of ocean transformed into a solid road beneath us. Behind us is the Red Sea. We look back at the past, and it gives us assurance for the future. God, who parted the sea behind me, is able to part the river before me. Although we can't see tomorrow, we know who holds tomorrow. God holds us too.

So no matter how unstable the road feels, we have security

because God has gone before us. He is our guide. Note that guidance and guides aren't the same. Directions on my phone provide me with guidance to my final destination. They can tell me where to go but can't walk beside me. They can point me in the right direction, but they won't keep my feet from slipping or quiet my fears around every sharp corner. Jesus *is* our guide. He does more than point us in the right direction; he *is* our direction. How do we know this? Because he calls himself our shepherd. And shepherds don't tell the sheep where to go; they lead the way. No road is unfamiliar to him because his breath spoke the world itself into existence. "Unfamiliar" is not a word in God's dictionary. There is no path he hasn't paved. He laid the foundation each one is built upon.

Have you ever been on a road that makes you want to turn around? The familiar back roads in my hometown don't make me feel that way because I've been there before. I know the curves of the road like the back of my hand. But unfamiliar roads? That's a whole different story. My husband and I decided to head home from Oregon to California via the scenic route of Highway 1. If you're unfamiliar with that two-lane coastal road, let me put it this way: There's a reason you can buy T-shirts that say, "I survived Highway 1." One of the most awe-inspiring but dangerous roads in the world—known for its landslides; narrow, cliff-hugging pavement; and windy turns—was our only route to our bed-and-breakfast. *Awesome.*

We left late in the day, not our best idea, and the night inevitably fell upon us, forcing us to traverse the rough terrain without the presence of daylight. With each sharp cliffside turn, I felt the winding road wind up fear within me. It's not that I didn't trust my husband—he's proven to be a very dependable driver—it's just that we had never traveled the road before. So what got us through? As much as the GPS guided us in the right direction, it was our headlights that led the way around every turn. Because the light was with us and before us, I knew we'd make it.

Jesus is not only our good shepherd but also the lamp to our feet and the light to our path on life's unfamiliar roads. He knows the way. He knows the way because he is the way. When you can't see up ahead, don't close your eyes and brace for what's ahead. Simply glance in the rearview mirror and believe God didn't bring you this far to leave you but to take you all the way.

One of the certainties of today is uncertainty. But one of the certainties of tomorrow is God. There's no reason to worry. We have absolute assurance: He will bring us home.

A TASTE OF
EMPOWERMENT

*"You shall hear what they say, and afterward your
hands shall be strengthened to go down against the
camp." Then he went down with Purah his servant to
the outposts of the armed men who were in the camp.*

JUDGES 7:11

Words have the power to fortify us. Your heart, soul, flesh,
and blood—yes, even your skin and bones—experi-
ence the power of words every day. Good news makes
you sigh with relief. An argument makes your face turn red. An
"I love you" makes your heart flutter.

Words and emotions have a symbiotic relationship so powerful they affect us on a cellular level. That means we must guard
our minds because what we believe to be true, the words we listen to and put weight behind, will take shape within our souls.

If I told you something that made your stomach drop but
then I immediately followed with "Just kidding," you most likely
wouldn't brush it off. Why? Because it felt real. You processed the
initial news or comment as truth, and the effect was set in motion.

The perceived reality, even for a sheer moment, was heavy enough on your heart to make you *feel* it.

God didn't distance himself from feelings but robed himself in humanity. He felt every drop of blood drip from his brow as he suffered the emotional turmoil of the coming cross. Resurrection was to come. But on the road there, the emotional and physical torment was real. The taunts and the nails made their full impact. He felt it all, from his hands to his heart. The duality of divine and human coincide in the person of Jesus. The outward reality of Calvary wasn't merely heavy on his heart; it completely crushed his spirit.

We can't deny the proverb "The light of the eyes rejoices the heart, and good news refreshes the bones" (Proverbs 15:30). When bad news reaches our ears, anxiety rolls in like a storm hitting the coastline. Is it possible to ever become like the one the psalmist wrote about? "He is not afraid of bad news; his heart is firm, trusting in the LORD" (Psalm 112:7). How are we able to stand strong in the face of our deepest trouble? A life filled exclusively with good news is of course a fairy tale, not reality. In the same way, a steady heart is not one that never gets rocked by turbulent waters but one that is anchored in the presence of the Savior during rising waves.

Gideon found this to be true when his army of 22,000 got thinned down to 300. Yikes. But look how God assured his heart in the middle of what seemed like bad news: "The people with you are too many for me to give the Midianites into their hand, lest Israel boast over me, saying, 'My own hand has saved me'"

(Judges 7:2). God just told him the battle was over before it began, but before the victory, God popped what could have inflated his false sense of strength. Then God filled Gideon's heart with the truth that *God alone is his strength*: "And you shall hear what they say, and afterward your hands shall be *strengthened* to go down against the camp" (Judges 7:11, emphasis added). He empowered Gideon with what? Words. God boosted his confidence and gave him the courage and assurance he needed to overcome his fear and trust God's strength to win the battle.

When your heart hears bad news, don't let worry weigh it down. The end of our understanding is not a ledge we fall off; it's a runway we surrender our grounding to in order to rise to new heights with God. So yes, we're refreshed by good news. But we're not *rescued* by good news. Even though "my flesh and my heart may fail . . . God is the strength of my heart and my portion forever" (Psalm 73:26). Take to heart when Jesus says "take heart" (John 16:33). Not because we'll never feel weak but because right in the middle of our weakness, he is found to be strong.

In the face of bad news, look to the face of the King. And when fear tries to shake you, remember his Word has already secured you; you can rise above every fear knowing he rose. Every fear is silenced by a love so loud it didn't have to say a word but went to a cross that gave him the last word: "It is finished" (John 19:30). May you let those words be the ground you stand on today, tomorrow, and into eternity.

A TASTE OF
ABUNDANCE

At mealtime Boaz said to her, "Come here and eat some bread and dip your morsel in the wine." So she sat beside the reapers, and he passed to her roasted grain. And she ate until she was satisfied, and she had some left over.

RUTH 2:14

Abundance attracts us. No wonder—by definition, abundance is an amount above and beyond what is needed to meet our basic needs. Who doesn't like the sound of that? Maybe you've noticed our world is quite fixated on abundance. Most of the time we think of abundance in terms of possessions. But a quick glance at Jesus's life tells a different story. Jesus's life dripped with abundance. Not in earthly belongings, but in his regular oversupply of meeting the needs of those around him. He knows our needs even in this moment, and wants to give us not *just enough* but to fill us above and beyond what we're capable of receiving. This is true for our basic needs and our deepest need—to be loved. He wants to fill our hearts with more than they could ever hold.

Because Jesus is generous in every way, we regularly see that his love cannot be contained and spills out as leftovers. When Jesus multiplied a kid's lunch of bread and fish to feed a hungry crowd of thousands, he provided so much food, they ate until they were stuffed and—you guessed it—had leftovers.

Boaz, who is like a picture of Jesus, invited Ruth to glean from his field and lightened the load of her work before she even set foot on his dirt. Boaz told his reapers to "pull out some stalks for her from the bundles and leave them for her to pick up" (Ruth 2:16 NIV). Ruth didn't have to pull the stalks; she just gathered bundles of blessing prepared in advance for her. Other workers might think that's undeserving or unfair. And they'd be exactly right. It's called grace, and grace is a gift. A gift can only be received, not worked for.

God is so abundantly generous with his love that it might even make you angry. Let me explain. One of my favorite scriptures that regularly fires me up is written by Luke: "But love your enemies, and do good, and lend, expecting nothing in return, and your reward will be great, and you will be sons of the Most High, for he is kind to the ungrateful and the evil" (Luke 6:35). Read that again. God is kind. To the ungrateful. And the evil. God's goodness rains on the just and the unjust because his love is not fair—it's free. For all. And this rain is not the unwanted kind that pours down when you're still a mile's walk away from your destination. It is the rain from heaven that brings growth to your land. God doesn't hold back the clouds on anyone.

Here's the catch . . . there is none. However, our desire for blessings can catch up to us if we're not careful. The shift can

GOD'S GOODNESS
rains on the just
and the unjust
because his love is
not FAIR — it's FREE.
For all.

happen before we realize it. One quick internet search for the word "abundance," and the first picture that shows up is a person with arms stretched out wide. Honestly, this is a pretty good picture of how we are to enjoy the blessings of God in this life: with open arms. Otherwise, our possessions become obsessions. Our blessings become binding.

The Bible says, "You shall remember the LORD your God, for it is he who gives you power to get wealth, that he may confirm his covenant that he swore to your fathers, as it is this day" (Deuteronomy 8:18). It's easy to skip over the last half of this verse, but it is important because it explains the *why*. What was the purpose of wealth? So God would confirm his covenant to Abraham. What was the covenant? That God was going to bless him. And that in return, Abraham would be a *blessing to others*.

This covenant didn't expire in the era of the Old Testament. This is exactly what Jesus does for us today. He blesses us and gives so generously, he gave his own life for us. He withheld nothing, not even himself. And because he gave, we are to give. We find abundant life when we realize it's Jesus we want—and him alone. Hold on to Jesus, and things won't hold on to you.

May you dance in the rain of God's blessings, and may they in turn make you look up and smile at the One who makes it rain.

A TASTE OF
FOCUS

The LORD said to Samuel, "Do not consider his appearance or his height, for I have rejected him. The LORD does not look at the things people look at. People look at the outward appearance, but the LORD looks at the heart."

1 SAMUEL 16:7 NIV

Eyes have a way of anchoring the soul.

My beach chair has become a familiar friend that I regularly plop down in the sand to have a front-row seat for the waves my husband, Bo, surfs. I plant myself right where he runs out into the ocean. I look down for a minute to read. A moment later, I look up to see the current has moved him down the beach. With a swivel of his head, he looks for the right direction: me. I'm his anchor. When his eyes are on the waves, he can easily get pulled out to sea, far away from where we originally intended to be. Where he looks is where he goes.

We must look to God to be the anchor of our souls. The momentum of the world is a rip current that daily pulls us away from the things of God. Unless we're paying attention, that is. Our part is to be intentional about where we fix our eyes. The world's pull is no more our fault than it was Eve's fault that the serpent came to tempt her with the fruit. We're born into a wild place, where underneath the calm is a hidden undertow of waves of deception that will carry us far from where God wants us to be. We must be careful not to be tossed around. We are bombarded with ideas that tempt us to believe them all day long. It's a fight to behold truth in a sea of deceit.

For many years, my eyes were anchored on my outward appearance. My goal was to move away from self-defeating thoughts that regularly washed over me: "I'm not good enough" or "I feel like a failure." I falsely believed that if I could change what I saw on the outside, then the lies on the inside would be silenced and no longer have power over me. But fixing my eyes on myself only made the problem worse. In the storms of life I learned that I'm not a good anchor for my soul. I got tossed around out there. Imagine if every time Bo looked at me, I moved my beach chair. It would be a never-ending paddle to nowhere. Only with God's help can we rise above the lies that pull us away from being anchored in the truth.

I soon discovered that God's Word cannot anchor our souls if it's not hidden in our hearts. Instead of listening to every voice that popped into my head, I took to heart what Paul wrote to the church of Corinth when he said, "We destroy arguments and every lofty opinion raised against the knowledge of God, and take every thought captive to obey Christ" (2 Corinthians 10:5). We swivel our head over to Jesus, then we paddle in the right direction. That doesn't mean the waves won't come. It doesn't mean there won't be undercurrents that try to draw us off course, but now we have a fixed anchor on the shore that's steadfast, unmovable, and the same yesterday, today, and forever (Hebrews 13:8).

Most of the time, I prefer to sit safely on the shore, but God has a way of calling us out. He places us in situations that challenge us to keep our focus where he is focusing. Like when God sent Samuel to the house of Jesse to anoint one of his sons to be king over Israel. Jesse brought out everyone except his youngest son, David, to stand before Samuel. God instructed Samuel not to look at their outward appearance but to look where he looks—the heart. Because his heart was anchored in God's, he had eyes to see that none who stood before him was God's chosen king. David's heart captured God's attention, and then God directed Samuel. May we, like Samuel, have a heart that's anchored in God, which will enable us to fix our eyes on the things of God. And may we, like David, not be afraid to step out when we're called away from our familiar shore. God will be our anchor. We'll never be pulled out to sea if we choose to see the One who will never lose sight of us.

A TASTE OF
DIRECTION

*Now, therefore, thus you shall say to my servant
David, "Thus says the LORD of hosts, I took you
from the pasture, from following the sheep, that
you should be prince over my people Israel."*

2 SAMUEL 7:8

I magine knowing what specific purpose God created you to fulfill. The good news is, there is no need to imagine it because
God wants to make it known to us. He wants us to go from
uncertainty to confidence, from confusion to clarity, from not
knowing who we are to being assured of whose we are. So let's do it.

We walk in the purpose for which we're created by walking
with our Creator. Nothing enriches our souls more than to walk
with God and enjoy life abiding in him, because a well-watered
soul makes a fruitful life. But you can't have fruit without the root,
and at the root of most of our dreams is the desire to reach the end
of our life and know we lived it well. We want to live with purpose and on purpose, but how do we do that? I'll never forget the
night my friend Alex dropped this one-liner: We won't know our
purpose until we know the One who gives life purpose. Bingo.

We start with knowing him. As extraordinary as it would be if a detailed, step-by-step map fell from heaven, we don't need that. The Maker of heaven lives inside us.

David, the shepherd boy turned king over Israel, asked God for clear, specific direction too: "Make me to know your ways, O LORD; teach me your paths" (Psalm 25:4). God ultimately took him from shepherding sheep to shepherding a nation. God's purpose was revealed for David as he walked hand in hand with his Maker. The same God who responded to David will respond to us, too, if only we'll recognize his voice. But that will only happen if we talk with him regularly. The first invitation Jesus actually gives us is to *follow*. Follow him. He said to repent, which means to do a 180-degree change of direction from walking our own path to following the way of Jesus. When we let him lead, we avoid the potholes of comparison, trying to be someone we're not, or worrying about what someone else is called to do instead of running our own race.

But what if you don't know what you're supposed to do? Not knowing is okay. You're not a failure if you can't figure out the way by yourself, because you weren't created to. That's like saying a child is a failure because they can't figure out their way to class on the first day of school. To them, the way to class is not "down the hall, take a left at the end, and it's the first door on the right." No. The way is found in the hand that holds their own. They need to lift up their hand to reach for their parent, *who is the way*.

Our Father showed us the way through his Son, Jesus. All we have to do is take his hand. Those directions might seem so uncomplicated, but it's true: We acknowledge God in all our ways, and *then* he will make our path straight (Proverbs 3:6). When we look to Jesus, the shifting sand under our feet turns to solid ground. He is our rock. He is our way: "The LORD makes firm the steps of the one who delights in him" (Psalm 37:23 NIV).

We can wish for a detailed map for our lives, or we can follow our good shepherd, who laid down his life for us. I think it's safe to say if he gave his life for ours, we can rest assured he'll lead us through this life. Of course, there might be times we think it would be cool for God to reveal his grand plan, down to every step and every turn, but honestly, wouldn't that make a boring journey home? It would be like watching the same movie every weekend. Even if you loved it, the story would get old. Let's surrender the writing of our story to him. We don't need to be afraid of the unknown, unwritten chapters because we know who holds the pen.

Delight in the journey with Jesus. Take his hand and he will lead you on the greatest adventure of your life while shaping you into the person you're supposed to be. Remember, God's biggest plan for the world came in a small, unassuming package. That baby from Bethlehem grew up to be the Lamb of God in order that he might become the way. May he give you eyes to see he's in the tiniest details of your life. May you allow the purpose of God to unfold in your life through the simple act of holding his hand. Let him lead you on the path he's set before you. Instead of reaching for a map, reach for his hand. And watch him direct your every step along a path rich in purpose. So don't worry. Just reach up your hand and start walking.

A TASTE OF
HUMANITY

*He lay down and fell asleep under a broom tree; but
behold, there was an angel touching him, and he said to
him, "Arise, eat!" And he looked, and behold, there was at
his head a round loaf of bread baked on hot coals, and a
pitcher of water. So he ate and drank, and lay down again.*

1 KINGS 19:5-6 NASB

Hangry is my least favorite mood. My words aren't always seasoned with grace when I find myself there. My soul agrees
with Paul when he said, "For I do not understand my own
actions. For I do not do what I want, but I do the very thing I
hate" (Romans 7:15). I think it's safe to say none of us wants to
snap at the people we love, but I do believe it is human to end up
depleted and not realize it until our actions remind us that our
basic needs have been neglected. Elijah is told by an angel to eat
some bread and take a nap. This story could be easy to pass by,
but if we slow down to savor it, we'll see it's a reminder that God
made us as human beings with basic needs, not spiritual robots.

God put within us dreams, desires, tendons, hunger, and emotions all wrapped up in this creation he calls "good." Because our

spirit resides in this temporary tent called a body, when we push our physical selves beyond what they can bear, it has an effect on our spirit. Sometimes we spiritually gloss over this important truth and then wonder why we're not able to walk in the Spirit when we're worn out or unnourished. Yes, we need the Spirit to help us even in our physical weakness, but we also find grace with our Father when we fall short.

That's why I appreciate how this part of Elijah's story is a clear reminder that as much as we are soul and spirit, we are also flesh and blood. This is not something God disregards but something he acknowledges: "For he knows our frame; he remembers that we are dust" (Psalm 103:14). And look at what the psalmist penned just before it: "As a father has compassion on his children, so the LORD has compassion on those who fear Him" (Psalm 103:13 NIV). I don't think our good Father would lash out at us in anger when we're hangry. It seems more like he'd make us a snack and do our chores while we nap. He knows we're dust; do we remember that too?

The more I study nutrition, the more clearly I see the fingerprints of God on everything. I see God in the sun that enables our bodies to synthesize vitamin D. I see him in the sunrise that allows our body to make hormones more energizing than coffee. When we don't eat for long periods of time, cortisol, a stress hormone, shoots through our body to keep us going. But if we'll pause and listen to our hunger signals when they speak, even they will point us to our perfect Creator. We avoid hangry and steady our mood by simply tuning into and respecting how we were made.

This might seem like a shallow topic, but my heart runs deep in the river of care. When my sister came to me newly postpartum, broken over how irritable she'd been, I didn't scold her and tell her to memorize James 1:19. I cleaned her house and made her lunch so she could nap.

We can't expect to have a healthy spirit if we regularly neglect the temple that houses it. And if we don't have helping hands giving us time to rest or an angel baking us a fresh loaf of bread, may we find grace in the arms of our Father who knows our frailty. So no, let's not use our bodies as excuses to sin, but maybe we should listen more carefully to the signals God put within these temporary tents of ours and remember the words of the angel to Elijah: "Arise, eat" (1 Kings 19:7 NASB). Leave the laundry and head for the kitchen. We are God's masterpiece, a masterpiece that needs a lot of carbs, protein, and grace. May we remember that God calls us higher, but when we fall, we'll find mercy and even a snack waiting.

A TASTE OF
DELIVERANCE

*Thus says the LORD, "You shall not see wind or rain,
but that streambed shall be filled with water, so that
you shall drink, you, your livestock, and your animals."
This is a light thing in the sight of the LORD.*

2 KINGS 3:17-18

D o you believe whatever you're stressed about is simple for God to handle? It's easy to doubt that an answer to prayer is on the way when it seems like help is nowhere in sight. *I'm gonna send you water*, God says, *but you won't see any rain.* By faith, we want to believe that everything is possible with God, but our logical brains pipe up and say, *Show me the nail prints, and then I'll believe* (John 20:25). We all like to laugh a little at Thomas in the Bible. We can't even say his name without inserting "doubting" before it. The reality is, most of us like proof too. A skepticism has settled down in our bones even though our hearts long to beat with faith.

It's hard to believe water is coming unless you see rain fall from the sky. It's hard to believe restoration is on the way when you're surrounded by brokenness. While a healthy dose of doubt can be a safeguard against deception, what happens to our souls when we regularly withhold faith from the One who alone is perfectly trustworthy? Hidden within plain sight of the promises of God is God himself. He is the promise keeper. And when we doubt what he's declared he'll do, it's never a broken promise that breaks us but broken faith that shakes us. To break a promise is to lie. And God has never lied. Maybe the problem is not that God is slow to deliver on his promises but that we're quick to lean on our own understanding. Because deliverance is coming. Whether we see it or not.

One day when Jesus was traveling with his disciples, he asked them who other people said he was. When they offered several responses, Jesus got to the heart of the issue: "What about you? Who do you say I am?" Peter's response hit the bullseye: "You are the Messiah, the Son of the living God." Peter was declaring that Jesus was the expected deliverer, the one who the Scriptures foretold was coming.

Jesus replied, "Blessed are you, Simon son of Jonah, for this was not revealed to you by flesh and blood, but by my Father in heaven. And I tell you that you are Peter, and on this rock I will build my church, and the gates of Hades will not overcome it" (Matthew 16:13-18 NIV).

Jesus goes on to tell his disciples how exactly deliverance would come: through the crucifixion and resurrection. He would suffer many things, be killed, and then be raised to life. *Whoa, whoa, whoa*, Peter must have thought. *You're the Christ! If you die, how will deliverance come?* And so Peter rebuked Jesus. Peter's eyes could not see deliverance coming through his Lord's death. That was not how he envisioned it.

Jesus turned to him and said, "Get behind me, Satan! You are a stumbling block to me; you do not have in mind the concerns of God, but merely human concerns" (Matthew 16:23 NIV). It kind of goes without saying that this isn't something you'd want to hear Jesus tell you.

Deliverance is coming whether we see it or not. Deliverance is coming whether we understand it or not. Deliverance is coming, and nothing can stop it, not even a cross. The word "deliver" literally means "to set free." Which is exactly what Jesus did at Calvary. He delivered us from evil. He set us free. Deliverance isn't found in the rain or in the way we think it should come; it's found where our hearts have closely held to their skepticism all along: the nail prints in his hands—the proof of freedom, found in the scars of our King. He will always make a way because he is the way. Whatever worry is holding your heart hostage, the ransom has come. Whatever you're stressed about is not insurmountable for God. Deliverance may come how we least expect it. Because nothing can stop the water from coming, not even a lack of rain.

A TASTE OF
PROSPERITY

You will prosper if you are careful to observe the statutes
and the rules that the LORD commanded Moses for Israel.
Be strong and courageous. Fear not; do not be dismayed.

1 CHRONICLES 22:13

Prosperity isn't an accident. It's a cultivation of doing. With God, we have more than the mere hope of a harvest but a guarantee of it. Imagine if the only thing a farmer had to do for a successful crop was to go out, stare at his crops, and call it a day. Doesn't exactly sound like a hard day of work, but that's exactly how God invites us into growth—by looking at him. Fruitfulness through observation might sound too good to be true; surely, the fruit of our labor must be accompanied by a little more sweat.

But if we take prosperity into our own hands, we'll find we're not strong enough to bear the weight of even the smallest seed.

At some point, every farmer must give up trust in themselves and realize that abundance isn't a willful act of control but a result of surrender to the One who waters the earth with rain. Prosperity is found when we look up. We're invited to simply *observe* God's law so we can flourish. And Jesus came as the fulfillment of the

Don't let your mind wander to thoughts that make you feel small, thoughts that make you wither. Bring your mind back to Jesus over and over to keep you **EVERGREEN.**

very law we're called to behold, which means we will thrive when we look at him.

Right before God brings his people into the land flowing with milk and honey, he describes how the soil there receives its nourishment: "The land which you go to possess is not like the land of Egypt from which you have come, where you sowed your seed and watered it by foot, as a vegetable garden; but the land which you cross over to possess is a land of hills and valleys, which drinks water from the rain of heaven, a land for which the Lord your God cares; the eyes of the Lord your God are always on it" (Deuteronomy 11:10-12 NKJV). This is not the water that people pump through irrigation pipes, but the rain dripped down from heaven's clouds. The promised land would drink of the abundance of God's poured-out provision, not of the sweat of their brow. He says, in effect, "I work, you rest. I'll keep my eyes on the land; you keep your eyes on me." We look up and let the rain wash away our self-sufficiency in the waters of perfect provision.

Look at what God says just after he promises nourishment from heaven: "Take care lest your heart be deceived, and you turn aside and serve other gods and worship them; then . . . he will shut up the heavens, so that there will be no rain, and the land will yield no fruit" (Deuteronomy 11:16-17). Fruitfulness is a by-product of endurance and a long-range focus. Looking at him roots us in fertile ground, just as the psalmist affirmed when describing the person who takes delight in the law of the Lord and meditates on it day and night: "He is like a tree planted by streams of water that yields its fruit in its season, and its leaf does not wither. In all that he does, he prospers" (Psalm 1:1-3).

One of the Hebrew words for meditation means "to ruminate" or "to chew on," like a cow chews its cud. We take in God's Word and savor it like a hard candy, letting it slowly dissolve. That's what happens when our eyes are constantly on Jesus: We find ourselves evergreen, prospering in all we do, dripping with abundance from heaven.

As we look at and to Jesus, we become like him. We follow his example by regularly talking with our Father and meditating on Scripture. The key to a prosperous life is to be in the Word and to look at the Word made flesh—Jesus—from the first light of day until your head hits the pillow at night. Don't let your mind wander to thoughts that make you feel small, thoughts that make you wither. Bring your mind back to Jesus over and over to keep you evergreen. Focus on thoughts that bring refreshment to your weary soul. That bring peace to your anxious mind. That give you hope for a fruitful tomorrow as you stay rooted and grounded in love. And watch yourself flourish as you simply let the rain fall with your eyes fixated on the wonder of heaven.

A TASTE OF
TRUST

*O our God, will you not execute judgment on them? For we
are powerless against this great horde that is coming against
us. We do not know what to do, but our eyes are on you.*

2 CHRONICLES 20:12

I don't know about you, but I don't like driving in fog. Driving
has its challenges even on sunny days, so throw in some pea-
soup fog, and the little control we do have goes out the window. We grip the wheel a little tighter, lean a little closer to the
dash, and basically turn into a snail on wheels. It's our nature to
vice grip whatever control we have left. But what about when this
happens in life? When something we love starts to slip from our
fingertips, when the path before us seems impossible, when we
can't see what's up ahead—do we hold on for dear life, or do we
let go and trust God?

It's easy to be gripped with fear when you start to lose your grip.
When I got a call from my father telling me he was being rushed
into emergency heart surgery, it felt like my world stopped. I wanted
nothing more than to be with him, but I was in Oregon, he was in
California, and the surgery was happening *now*. The doctors did

51

not sugarcoat the severity of the situation; by their evaluation, my dad shouldn't be alive. Geography separated us, and every fiber of my being wished that wasn't so. No matter how fast I traveled, it wouldn't be fast enough. I'd like to tell you that I calmly surrendered my fear to God, but the truth is that fear and faith pulled me back and forth and waged a tug-of-war within my soul. It was at that moment I realized the only thing we have control over in this life is if we'll choose to trust God.

My eyes were opened to see that control is nothing more than an illusion. Of course, we have control over certain decisions, and we have to take responsibility for our actions, but when circumstances roll in like a fog and make us unable to see up ahead, what do we do? Do we throw our hands up in defeat, or do we lift them higher to find the One our help comes from?

Moses's mother let go of her son not knowing if she would ever see him again (Exodus 2). Watching her baby float down the river, I'm sure fear flooded her mind. What gave her the courage to let go? Maybe she realized peace doesn't come from control but from God. The peace God gives doesn't argue with our minds because it's busy guarding our hearts. It's easy to imagine the thought of "what ifs" clouding her vision and paralyzing her with fear. The unknown future of what would happen to Moses downriver was scary enough. But with Pharaoh's order to murder all newborn males, the future would be sealed if she held on to her baby—it would surely result in her son's death. She chose to put her trust in God, who would not only make a way for her baby down the river but also one day use that newborn boy to part the Red Sea.

The story reminds us that God isn't a "just enough" kind of God. He always does immeasurably more than we could ask or think. Maybe the path before you today feels impossible. I think it's easy to feel like we're failing God when we give in to fear rather than leaning into faith. Fear doesn't need permission to take over when we can't see up ahead. When the unimaginable call comes through. When the unthinkable news hits your ears. Fear didn't need permission to take over when my dad was rushed into surgery. But I needed to give God permission to perform surgery. Not on my dad—on me. I needed God to remove from my heart the fear of losing control. Imagine what we'll gain when fear of the unknown no longer has a grip on us. More room to breathe. More room to trust. Room for surgery that feels scary but will save your life. Whenever your heart is thick with the fog of improbability, remember that God has never met an impossibility.

A TASTE OF
JESUS

Ezra had set his heart to study the Law of the LORD,
and to do it and to teach his statutes and rules in Israel.

EZRA 7:10

Opening the Scriptures opens up a whole new world. A world of doctrine. History. Theology. An endless ocean we can swim in for a lifetime with more undiscovered riches waiting for us. While we can fish for the mysteries of God forever, the greatest treasure is one that's not hidden: "You search the Scriptures because you think that in them you have eternal life; and it is they that bear witness about me" (John 5:39). That's Jesus-talk for "at the bottom of the glass of Scripture is me." When we explore the Word of God, we are exploring Jesus, the heart of God.

Of course, Jesus isn't telling us not to study or know Scripture. In fact, his life shows the opposite. At the early age of twelve, he is in the temple listening and asking questions. As he matured, the law is clearly written in his heart because it's so quick on his tongue. Not to mention, *he* is the Word with skin on: "And the Word became flesh and dwelt among us, and we have seen his glory, glory as of the only Son from the Father, full of grace and truth" (John 1:14). We can't separate Jesus from the Word because he is the Word.

When we look at the Bible exclusively through the lens of acquiring head knowledge or shaping doctrine, perhaps it's not a lens at all but a lid that keeps our eyes from seeing the most important secret hidden in plain sight: the resurrected heart that beats behind the Word itself, Jesus the Son of God.

The Bible is a telescope. And when we can't clearly see the greatest mystery of God, that he made himself known to us through his Son Jesus, it's not that he's hiding; it's that we're not looking correctly. Maybe it sounds a little lofty to claim there's a right and wrong way to view Scripture, but no one would ever say that about something that's objective, like me looking *at* a telescope rather than *through* it. Everyone would agree there's a right and wrong way to use it. The tool's purpose is not to be looked at but to open up a whole new world when we look through it. That is what happens when we look at Scripture through the lens of Jesus: A window to the heavens opens.

The religious elite of Jesus's time looked at the telescope rather than through it. They missed eternal life even though he walked right in front of them. They knew Scripture. They quoted Scripture. But they studied the telescope so much, they never used it to look up at the heavens. Jesus is the way to the Father. Just before his earthly mission is accomplished, you can hear the beat of Jesus's heart for us in his prayer: "And this is eternal life, that they know you, the only true God, and Jesus Christ whom you have sent" (John 17:3). Eternal life is found in knowing Jesus, and we get to know him through the telescope of Scripture. In using the telescope for its intended purpose, our eyes are opened to see what's impossible to behold without it.

Most of us get lost at some point on the path of life. God knew we would. So he sent Jesus to show us the way back to him. Scripture reveals that Jesus is the way, so no matter how far you've wandered or how lost you feel, it's never too late to reroute or ask for directions: "Stand by the roads, and look, and ask for the ancient paths, where the good way is; and walk in it, and find rest for your souls" (Jeremiah 6:16). Open the Word, then look up. You'll find home isn't very far—it's only a prayer away.

A TASTE OF
STRENGTH

*Then he said to them, "Go your way. Eat the fat and
drink sweet wine and send portions to anyone who has
nothing ready, for this day is holy to our Lord. And do
not be grieved, for the joy of the LORD is your strength."*

NEHEMIAH 8:10

The most important thing we can ever do is to never give
up, even though our hearts are regularly wearied by heavy
things. Sickness. Crisis. Worry. Fear. Regret. Loss. Discour-
agement. And in some seasons, it seems that's only the beginning
of the list, a list that can become too long and full of things too
heavy to carry. Some days, our strength runs out the door bright
and early and, with it, our joy too. We hear, "And let us not grow
weary of doing good, for in due season we will reap, if we do not
give up" (Galatians 6:9). But how do we muster the strength to
carry on? Maybe *we* don't.

I'll never forget the day I was enjoying an afternoon on the
beach when a little boy walked by and caught my eye. On top of
his little head, he wore the biggest, floppiest sun hat you've ever
seen. Or rather, it was wearing him. I smiled as I watched his father

carry him as he played peekaboo with the brim of the huge hat. All of a sudden, it hit me how often we do that in life. We take on these oversized responsibilities, things that feel twice our size. We know we're too small to be wearing them. They don't fit right, and a mirror doesn't need to show it because we already know it. We feel the weariness like a weight inside our souls.

I want to remind you just as God reminded me on the beach that day: When we carry stuff that's too big for us, we have a Father who carries us. The reality is, life *is* too heavy for us. The good news is, the end of our strength isn't the end of our story. When we lift up what's wearing us down to meet our Father's eyes, we can relax because we remember whose hands we're in. We're yoked up with God in this life. He shoulders the weight of it all for us and with us. We avoid exhaustion when we release our worry to a compassionate Father. We'll only be tempted to give up if we believe we go at life alone. Kids? They're *never* alone. And neither are we because that's exactly who we are—God's kids.

May the reality that we are children of God sink into our souls in a way that changes us. The hat was way too big for the little boy. He couldn't see his way over the sand. But his dad carried him. And that's what made all the difference. He is our strength. We don't carry it all alone. So take your burdened heart to the One whose joy it is to be your strength. Run into the Father's arms, and you'll find he delights in carrying you. It's his joy that fortifies the fibers of our soul, that makes us resilient to weariness, a strength not found within ourselves but in him alone. You will never weary the heart of God by bringing your burdens to him because he waits every day to pick you up, put you onto his shoulders, and take care of all the heavy lifting for you. In our weakness, he remains who he is. Strong. Every step of the way, every single day.

We need never be ashamed that our hearts aren't strong enough to lift the burdens of this life, because they were never created to shoulder that kind of weight. We're kids, and kids of course don't carry heavy things—they get carried. One of the most powerful lies our enemy can make us believe is that we aren't God's children. Let's allow our fears to be calmed in the arms of our Father. And may we get back to simply being his kids, full of trust and laughter and without worry or care, because we're right where we belong: in the arms of the Father, whose joy it is to raise us up. So don't ever give up, not because you'll never get tired but because he'll never tire of carrying you.

A TASTE OF
PURPOSE

If you keep silent at this time, relief and deliverance will rise for the Jews from another place, but you and your father's house will perish. And who knows whether you have not come to the kingdom for such a time as this?

ESTHER 4:14

Do we greet unexpected moments in life with a welcoming hello? When we're introduced to moments we'd rather not face, we meet more than the moment—we meet *ourselves.* Coming face-to-face with who we are is something we'd probably shy away from rather than step into. Perhaps it's because where we'd like to see faith, we see fear. Where we'd like to see trust, we see worry. When we'd like to feel strong, we feel weak.

Maybe the moment you've arrived at today has left you feeling unprepared and powerless. What if this moment is not an accident but an appointed opportunity? What if it's not a dead end but an invitation to open the door of purpose? "For such a time as this" is one of the most beloved and quoted scriptures and is typically associated with a serendipitous moment. But how did Esther view the time playing out in front of her? Through eyes of favor, feeling divinely chosen to rise to the occasion? Perhaps the story sheds a different light on its meaning.

Esther faced a dilemma when a new law threatened to be the end of the Jewish nation if she didn't speak up. The problem was that she'd have to risk her life to save theirs. Esther didn't want to go before the king, so Mordecai scolded her: "Who knows whether you have not come to the kingdom for such a time as this?" (Esther 4:14). This was hardly an endearing moment. Esther's "for such a time as this" was a rebuke for considering her own safety over the lives of countless others. In the end, she decided to face the king with the declaration "If I perish, I perish" (Esther 4:16), which was likely said with bone-chilling fear in her soul rather than courage in her heart. God worked a great victory through Esther by calling her to devotion to a kingdom higher than her own. As we look carefully at Queen Esther, we catch a glimpse of King Jesus.

As Jesus knelt with a heavy heart to pray in the garden during the final moments before he faced the cross, he, too, arrived at the hour for which he had come. Esther was spared and saved a whole nation. Jesus was *not* spared and saved the whole world. This was the moment he came for. His royal moment was not wrapped in pleasure but robed in pain. This was his moment to be lifted up, not on a pedestal but on a cross. His time to be crowned not with gold but with thorns. His moment, too, of a sorrow that filled his soul: "Going a little farther he fell on his face and prayed, saying, 'My Father, if it be possible, let this cup pass from me; nevertheless, not as I will, but as you will'" (Matthew 26:39). Even with grief, he was able to endure the road to Calvary because of the joy set before him. He didn't think of himself first but instead laid his body down to swing wide the doors of salvation for you and me, a sacrifice that created the way to his kingdom, not of this world but for this world. This surrender-turned-victory didn't end in the grave but with the beating heart of our risen king.

When our "such a time as this" moment arrives, may we recognize it even if it's not wrapped in a bow. If we try to live a life free of pain, we'll of course find we can't escape it. But if we see the purpose in our pain, we'll find that a life well lived won't escape us. Perhaps the most fulfilling thing we'll ever do is be emptied of ourselves. If we live for ourselves, we wear nothing more than a perishable crown. May we surrender to our purpose and hear Jesus say, "Whoever seeks to preserve his life will lose it, but whoever loses his life will keep it" (Luke 17:33). Because with Jesus, to live is Christ and to die is gain (Philippians 1:21).

A TASTE OF
NOURISHMENT

*I have not departed from the commandment
of his lips; I have treasured the words of his
mouth more than my portion of food.*

JOB 23:12

Where else would we go except for food when we're hungry? It's hard to forget our obvious physical needs, yet when it comes to spiritual hunger, it seems we either forget to fill up or we don't know where to go for nourishment. While we know Job is being poetic, the gravity of his statement pulls us in with curiosity. Job said he treasures the words of God more than his daily bread. This is the beating heart behind his radically beautiful statement: God is better than life itself—he *is* life. He is the breath in our lungs. Every heartbeat belongs to him.

Job pushes beyond the here and now and gives us an appetite for the eternal life we have in Christ, where our soul awakens to the wonder of heaven. Hold on, though—I can't do anything, including treasure the words of God's mouth, unless I'm alive. So food is kind of important, right? But this is *exactly* what Job paints for us: To live without the daily Word of God inside our souls is

**We can simply LIVE,
or we can come ALIVE
to our real life in God.
We need daily bread
both for our LIPS
and for our SOULS.**

like trying to live without daily food inside our stomachs. We can't survive without it. We can't walk away from food without leaving life itself on the table. And in the same way, we can simply live, or we can *come alive* to our real life in God. We need daily bread both for our lips and for our souls.

Our search for sustenance ends with Jesus. As Peter said, "Lord, to whom shall we go? You have the words of eternal life" (John 6:68). Where else would we go except to food when we're hungry, and where else would we go for life except to the words of Jesus?

Jesus shared the same idea when he quoted Deuteronomy during his time of fasting and temptation in the wilderness: "Man shall not live by bread alone, but by every word that comes from the mouth of God" (Matthew 4:4). What if we know this to be true with our head but not our heart? Do we treasure the words of Jesus as the ultimate source of life? What if we don't currently crave regular time in God's Word? If we're honest with ourselves, are we hungry for him? And if we're not, how do we change that?

Well, you crave what you regularly consume, so what you currently crave is a good indicator of your present diet. If you don't want to crave fast food, then stop eating it, and you'll stop craving it. If you want to start craving nourishing food, you know what you have to do. We lose our appetite for the things we don't frequently chew on—whether it's deeply nourishing or not so much. The way we can regularly hunger to be in the Word of God is to make it a regular part of our diet. We must choose to put it on our plates daily to lead our cravings in the direction we want them to go.

The most harmful influence our enemy could have is to make

us lose our appetite for the Word of God. Fight to stay hungry! We live in a world that craves the "good life" but will fill up on everything but life itself. That's because the world treasures passing pleasure rather than real nourishment. Let's not be fooled into settling for bread alone. May our souls be ravenous for life, and if life feels empty, perhaps it's because we've filled up on everything but life himself: "I am the bread of life; whoever comes to me shall not hunger, and whoever believes in me shall never thirst" (John 6:35). Believe in Jesus and you'll have life. Come to him daily and you'll never hunger again. May we eat and be satisfied and find that satisfaction is only the beginning of what the Word made flesh provides for us. He'll direct our steps and fill us with purpose, joy, and peace—and that's only the start of a very long list of what comes with a life fully nourished in him. Let's make room on our plates for treasure and find we never again settle for bread alone.

A TASTE OF
LIGHT

Those who look to him are radiant, and
their faces shall never be ashamed.

PSALM 34:5

As I went on a sunset walk one evening, I gazed at the golden beams and wondered why we're so drawn to the sun. It seems the warm glow from the rays unearths a part of us that longs for the light. For many years I was tempted to believe radiance was found in the mirror. I thought if I could see myself in a way that made me approve of my body, my life would be better. Happier. Filled with sunshine. But the more I looked to my reflection to draw out the things I wanted most, the further the light was drawn out of me.

When something sparkles, our eyes can't help but be drawn to it. A better body? A better ____? The options to fill in that blank are endless, but the promises each of them makes are empty. This is the lie at the heart of the serpent's deception all the way back in Eden: "You will not surely die. For God knows that when you eat of it your eyes will be opened, and you will be like God, knowing good and evil" (Genesis 3:4-5). The serpent's lies fill Eve with doubt, and she debates whether she should take a bite. She wonders, *Maybe God is withholding good from us? Maybe satisfaction is just out of reach? Maybe God can't be trusted?* I gave in just as Eve did. But instead of eating fruit, I restricted it.

Instead of trusting, we become controlling. We let go of our trust in God so we can grip the illusion of control. We take matters into our own hands, quite literally, trying to draw nourishment from something that isn't created to satisfy. And we find it's shiny but shallow. It promises us wealth but makes us poor in what matters. It promises us happiness but robs us of joy. It promises us the world, but we lose our souls.

How do we break free?

We simply step into the light.

The light of God's love loosens deception's grip on us. It highlights truth, illuminating every desire that lures us into an empty promise. We don't have to go halfway and turn around, because he told us at the trailhead, *You won't find what you're looking for here.* And yet when we ignore his direction and inevitably get lost, he will never tell us to take a hike. He will always embrace us and never shame us. When I ran to the mirror with the goal of finding satisfaction, no matter how hard I looked, it was never there. I'd go right back to the treadmill to quiet the voice in my head assuring me satisfaction was just around the corner if only I ran a little faster. The problem was no matter how fast I ran, the elusive finish line outran me.

Finally, weariness overtook my stubbornness. I stopped my running and ran back into the arms of grace, who didn't push me away in shame but embraced me in love. It was there all along, not *something* I needed to find but *someone* who found me. And his name wasn't satisfaction but Jesus, who held that very thing in his hand.

When we look in the mirror, it seems like shame is never far away; fears, failures, and lies try to prove that's who we are. But when we look at Jesus, despite our sin, shame is nowhere to be found. It's all silenced in the light of his love. The light of the world who looked upon our darkness went to the cross, despising the shame, so that we might look to him and be radiant. May we find radiance not in the mirror but in the face of our King, who was put to shame so we'd never be.

PROVERBS

A TASTE OF
SWEETNESS

*Gracious words are like a honeycomb, sweetness
to the soul and health to the body.*

PROVERBS 16:24

D o we really believe that words have the power to nourish us? That they can touch our souls with sweetness like honey and, as calcium does, bring health to our bones? If there's anything we can say about Jesus, it's that his words hold power. Power to speak the universe into existence, bring sight to the blind, and put words in the mouths of those who had never uttered any. The people who lived to hear the words of Jesus in real time were amazed at his teachings because of his authority, but what made them *marvel* were the gracious words he spoke. So while our words will never hang stars in space, they do have the power to nourish.

As I sat happily working away in my favorite coffee shop, I heard the barista being genuinely kind to everyone as they placed their drink orders. I could feel the warmth inside me, without even taking a sip from my hot latte. Her words weren't spoken directly to me, yet I could *feel* the goodness. As I went about my day and headed over to the local farm stand, the warm smiles and kind exchanges between employees and customers made me feel it again: a sweetness inside me before I even had a chance to bite into the perfectly ripe strawberries I had just purchased.

What is this feeling? Just happiness? Perhaps it's something deeper. *Nourishment?* Yes, that's it. As I loaded the fresh produce into my car, I watched the sunset cast beams through the evening clouds and thought about the amount of honeycomb, as Proverbs calls it, I had eaten that day. I felt *full.* Stuffed to the brim and satisfied with gracious words. Words that are filled with life are as energizing to our souls as glucose is to our cells. And if they have the capability to nourish, they also have the potential to do the opposite.

I later found myself back in my favorite coffee shop, and a sweet elderly woman sat down next to me and offered a warm smile. As I responded in kindness, she proceeded to ask me what drink I ordered. "It's a spiced butterscotch latte. You should try it! It's seasonal, so it will be gone soon." She looked down at her cappuccino with what seemed like regret, got up, and returned a few minutes later with you know what in hand. She felt the need to assure me that she would skip lunch, and without hesitation, I smiled and shook my head, kindly but firmly assuring her, "Don't skip lunch. Enjoy your latte *and* your lunch."

I had heard her mindset before. Her words were reminiscent of my own—of the years I spent restricting food and speaking words that did anything but nourish my soul. I thought harsh words would motivate me to be more self-controlled. I listened to my own critical voice above the gracious words of God. I experienced what James describes: "With the tongue we praise our Lord and Father, and with it we curse human beings, who have been made in God's likeness" (James 3:9 NIV). I had been cursing someone who had been made in the image of God: *myself.* It hit me like a ton of bricks. How can we love our neighbor as ourselves if we don't love ourselves? Not a love of self that fills us with pride but a love that empties us because we've been filled with truth.

How can I tell my friend to enjoy her latte and lunch if I won't first let God's love into my own heart in a way that spills over onto my plate? From your words to your food, let love in so deep you're not afraid to jump high because your foundation is firm. Not a superficial self-love but a soul-grounding security in *his* love. Drink your latte. Enjoy your lunch. And more than that, be nourished by the gracious words of Jesus. We love because he first loved us. We nourish others because we have been nourished. Let's be generous in giving out gracious words to others and find that they fill us up too.

A TASTE OF
PATIENCE

He has made everything beautiful in its time. Also, he has
put eternity into man's heart, yet so that he cannot find
out what God has done from the beginning to the end.

ECCLESIASTES 3:11

I've never met someone who likes being a work in progress. Given the choice, most of us want to cross the finish line as quickly and painlessly as possible to enjoy the promise and satisfaction completion brings. We even do this at the grocery store: Which line do we choose? The longest of course. (Didn't see that coming, did you?) Of course not. We would *never* do that. But if you are someone who willfully chooses to do small, everyday things to let patience have its perfecting work in you, well, you have my respect . . . and you should probably be the one writing this book instead of me. Seriously! Patience is a fruit of the Spirit that seems to grow quite slowly on my tree.

I'm being lighthearted, but I know that patience is a real struggle. It's uncomfortable for all of us. We really do want to be patient, but impatience seems to war with that good intention. How do

73

we allow patience to flourish in our lives? Maybe we should start at the root of the fruit.

First Corinthians says, "Love is patient and kind" (13:4), so it seems that patience will be a direct result of a life deeply rooted in love. Actually, Scripture paints this out for us and invites us to be "rooted and grounded in love" (Ephesians 3:17). The question then is not *How do I become more patient?* but *How do I grow deeper in love?* It's interesting that roots are opportunistic—they don't just grow by accident in random directions; they intentionally look for ways to grow. They search for where they can draw nutrients and water from the soil. If they don't seek what they need, they don't grow. Could the same be true for us?

What does this practically look like in our lives? How do we look for opportunities for love to grow in our souls? What are we even supposed to look for? The Scripture tells us exactly: "By this we know love, that he laid down his life for us, and we ought to lay down our lives for the brothers" (1 John 3:16). There we go: Love will look for opportunities to lay its life down in service for others. That's how it grows. If we want to become patient, this is how we do it.

Jesus often used examples from the natural world to teach us spiritual truths. Just as he said, "Look at the birds of the air" (Matthew 6:26), we can imagine him saying, "Look at the roots." We watch how roots grow and do as they do. We mimic them. We look for ways to love others how Jesus loved us, by crucifying impatience in pursuit of being kind to others, because that's what love does: Kindness pulls out the weeds of selfishness.

Now, notice that love specifically couples patience and kindness. This combination is not random. When does unkindness usually spill out of us most easily? When we're being impatient. How do we treat the people we love when we are in a hurry or when we want them to hurry? That right there is an opportunity (or a million) to grow.

But remember, every time we miss the opportunity to grow is not a time God will speak to us harshly; it's an opportunity for God to nourish the soil of our hearts with his rich grace. He is patient with us. He is kind to us. So take heart: just because we don't see fruit right away doesn't mean we're not growing. Remember, there is no shortcut to growth, so let's allow ourselves to be roots in progress.

A TASTE OF
LOVE

I adjure you, O daughters of Jerusalem, that you not stir up or awaken love until it pleases.

SONG OF SOLOMON 8:4

To awaken love implies that love has fallen asleep. I wish I could sit down with you and listen to you pour out your heart because I don't know how you feel about love or how you'd describe the current condition of your heart. Maybe your love life didn't turn out as planned; the love that once awakened your heart now makes you wish you'd stayed asleep. Maybe you're in love, but it sure doesn't feel the same as it did in the beginning. Maybe you feel as though you've waited an eternity for someone's love to wake up and find you. Or maybe you can say, as King Solomon did, that you've found the One whom your soul loves. No matter your relationship status, our greatest need for love is to love God and be loved by him. And it is never too early in life to be awakened by this love.

We're put on this earth to love God with everything we are. And until our souls awaken to that, we go through life asleep. That sleepiness spills over into our relationships with others too.

76

In fact, that's the other side of the pillow: to love God and love your neighbor as yourself. One of my favorite moments of Jesus's life is when one of the scribes asks him which commandment is the most important of all. Jesus answered him: "You shall love the Lord your God with all your heart and with all your soul and with all your mind and with all your strength." But he doesn't stop there. He continues, "The second is this: 'You shall love your neighbor as yourself.' There is no other commandment greater than these" (Mark 12:30-31). Notice Jesus's singular use of the word "commandment," not "commandments." He views loving God and loving people as one and the same. In loving others, we love God—they are two sides of the same coin. You simply can't separate loving God from loving others.

But here's the kicker: The scribe responds, "You are right, Teacher. You have truly said that he is one, and there is no other besides him. And to love him with all the heart and with all the understanding and with all the strength, and to love one's neighbor as oneself, is much more than all whole burnt offerings and sacrifices." That last sentence is what makes Jesus's head turn. I picture a smile rising at the corner of Jesus's mouth as he validated the scribe's words: "You are not far from the kingdom of God" (Mark 12:34).

I could soak in those words all day. The scribe was onto something. He almost touched the kingdom with his mention of love being greater than burnt offerings and sacrifices. The kind of love God wants from us is not based on our performance. The world wants our performances. It likes a good show and applauds those who know how to play the part and draw the spotlight to themselves through their actions and words. If we pursue that self-serving path and then say "Praise the Lord!" we might fool other people, but we can't fool God. He doesn't want a good show; he wants our hearts to beat after his. He wants you to pray your raw prayer, not for you to pretend everything's okay. He wants to hear from you throughout the day, not just once a week on a Sunday. He doesn't want us to play the part in front of people to appear close to him when all along our heart is distant or even resistant. He wants the core of who we are, our heart. The uncut version of us, not the person we think we need to be for him to love us. His love isn't earned, so we don't have to give out what isn't real anyway. Instead we live with a wide-open heart and let the love of God rain down on us. Then we pour it out on others.

What gets us close to the kingdom? A real love for God. The love we cultivate for God then flows out onto people. No matter what your heart is longing for today, know this—God's love for you is not asleep in the grave but alive in Jesus. May our sleepy hearts so awaken to the real, raw love of God that they never want to go back to bed.

A TASTE OF
TRANSFORMATION

*O LORD, you are our Father; we are the clay, and you
are our potter; we are all the work of your hand.*

ISAIAH 64:8

I don't volunteer my heart to carry heavy things. Nevertheless, they get placed there sometimes. When we imagine growing into who God created us to be, it seems we forget about the growing pains. We're not hardwired for the pain that came with the curse; we long for Eden before the fall and feel the ache for perfection deep within our bones. But let's not be afraid for these bones to grow, even if it means enduring some pain in the night, because one day, the sun will rise and never set. We're being shaped for eternity, so though our hearts sometimes carry heavy things, the strength these burdens produce in us prepares us to someday carry unending joy.

One evening, I woke up in the middle of the night after receiving news earlier that day that completely crushed my spirit. I made my way to the kitchen with teary eyes, feeling like my heart was trying to lift a thousand pounds. My single goal right then was to make it through the night somehow. Would I make it to dawn by finally sleeping or by staying awake with the help of caffeine? I contemplated what I should do as I looked at my favorite monstera-designed mug sitting on the open shelf. *Should I pour some coffee?* My sleepy, throbbing head somehow stopped thinking about caffeine and took notice of this custom-made pottery created by my artist friend who hand-shaped it. I thought about how this beautiful mug, my *favorite* mug, started out as a lump of clay. In that state, it wasn't this pretty or useful. Until it landed in the potter's hands.

It honestly doesn't sound very comfortable to be a lump of clay that is pressed down, thrown around, smoothed out, and then ultimately placed into a fire. The process of becoming a useful, beautiful creation includes immense pressure and blazing heat because the clay has no ability to become anything until it yields to the potter's hands. If that clay were in my hands, it would never turn into a mug; it would remain nothing more than a wet lump of mud. Why? Because I'm not an artist. But in the right hands? It is transformed into a useful and beautiful piece of art.

We can trust that in God's hands, we'll be made into all we were created to be.

As I stood in the kitchen with my head spinning, I realized, *I'm on the potter's wheel.* Not everything that happens to us is good. And not everything in us is good either. As we yield to the hands of the potter, what comes out of our hard-pressed hearts? Frustration? Impatience? Bitterness? Being quick to anger? Maybe all the above. But may we remember that although we see the finished work only when it's finally on the shelf, the potter's eyes see a

The potter's eyes see a MASTERPIECE in the middle of the mud. God will complete the work he begins in us because he sees the MIRACLE, not the mess.

masterpiece in the middle of the mud. God will complete the work he begins in us because he sees the miracle, not the mess. He sees the completed work from the start. May we remember that even Jesus surrendered himself to the hands of the Father, and may his prayer be on our lips too: "Not my will, but yours" (Luke 22:42). Jesus yielded to the weight of the cross, and when hard-pressed, what came out of him? Perfect love.

I don't volunteer my heart for heavy things, but Jesus did in order that he might lift the burdens off ours. We are being molded and transformed into the image of the One whose heart was crushed for ours, so our hearts might also take the shape of perfect love.

How could an artist ever leave the clay to itself, knowing the possibilities in their hands are endless? We are the clay. He is the potter. May we recognize trials as times we're being worked on because we're clay. Let's not let our hearts be weighed down by the pressure, but let's take heart, knowing whose hands we're in.

A TASTE OF
HOPE

*I know the plans I have for you, declares the LORD, plans for
welfare and not for evil, to give you a future and a hope.*

JEREMIAH 29:11

O ne of the most famous promises of the Bible is found right
in the middle of one of Israel's darkest nights. It was shared
to give hope during the worst of days. God made this declaration of the good plans he has for Israel, not at a high point but
while they were being forced into exile. I'm sure they thought, *Did
we hear you right? Do you see what is happening to us?*

In what appears to be a sky of hopelessness, God's promise
breaks through the clouds as a glimmer of light. He says he has
plans for their welfare, which Webster's defines as "the state of doing
well especially in respect to good fortune, happiness, well-being,
or prosperity." Honestly, they might have looked around in confusion and thought God was kidding. God tells them of goodness
ahead as they're cut off from their land of milk and honey to live in
a place not their own. What? Here's the paradox: "God has made
me fruitful in the land of my affliction" (Genesis 41:52). It would
be a lot more fun to say God has made me fruitful in the land of

my blessing. But the mystery is that God blesses us in the land of hardship because God himself makes us fruitful, not the land.

Years ago, when I felt pressure to get a "perfect body," I over-exercised and underate. My goal was health. Yet the closer I tried to get to it, the further away from actual health I got. I found myself deep in the pit of an eating disorder with what seemed like no way out. I've never met anyone who likes to live in the land of hardship, but knowing you placed yourself there is additionally painful. God not only rescued me but redeemed my story too. I can look back in the review mirror of my life and see God's good hand. What the psalmist penned is true through every season and soil: "He is like a tree planted by streams of water that yields its fruit in its season, and its leaf does not wither. In all that he does, he prospers" (Psalm 1:3). We can be evergreen even in the land of affliction because goodness grows where God is.

Joseph also found this to be true, though a peek into his life makes you want to look away. He often found himself in pits and prisons. Injustice was around every corner including betrayal by his own brothers, yet we read over and over that the Lord was with him. And whatever Joseph did or faced, God made him succeed. That doesn't shout success to me though—to be taken advantage of and mistreated, with your reputation dragged through the mud and a chunk of your innocent life gone behind bars. Neverthe-less, this rugged road leads Joseph before Pharaoh, where he's ele-vated from prisoner to prime minister, enabling him to save not only his brothers who betrayed him but every person affected by the widespread famine. Joseph declared to the ones who set him on this tumultuous journey that what they meant for evil, God meant for good. Talk about redemption.

Of course, it's not that bad things won't ever happen to us, but when they do, God still works it out for good. Why? Because we love him (Romans 8:28). There are no dead ends with God. We can look back and see that every wrong turn has led us where we're supposed to be, not because we're good at directions but because God is good at redeeming. Surely, his goodness and mercy follow us all the days of our life, even in the land of affliction. We don't need to be afraid of where we are. Instead, we must trust the One who's with us. God is in this land making all things, even the unlikely, work together for our good. No matter where we find ourselves in life, we'll come to a place where in *every* place we can say, "Surely the LORD is in this place, and I did not know it" (Genesis 28:16).

A TASTE OF
MERCY

The steadfast love of the LORD never ceases;
his mercies never come to an end; they are new
every morning; great is your faithfulness.

LAMENTATIONS 3:22-23

Just as God does not withhold the sunrise at the beginning of each new day, so too, new mercies faithfully rise to greet us alongside the sun. And God does more than give out fresh mercy in the morning. He actually *feels* merciful toward us. Mercy is both in his hand and in his heart. He gives it and he is it. God is rich in mercy, a gift he wants to give out of the nature of who he is. And it's a gift we desperately need. Why? Because without it, our souls will never be able to stand up straight. In Paul's words, "For all have sinned and fall short of the glory of God" (Romans 3:23). Sin is *hamartia* in Greek, which means "to miss the mark." Picture an arrow not hitting the bull's-eye. We take our aim and miss. We run through life and fall—not just once but every day. But guess what waits around every corner? Fresh mercy. So much of it that it flows down from heaven as a never-ending rainstorm from a God who's eager to open the clouds.

Mercy means we don't get what we deserve. We deserve the results of our aim. We sinned. Didn't hit the target. So how do the results come in? "For the wages of sin is death, but the free gift of God is eternal life in Christ Jesus our Lord" (Romans 6:23). We're not on the receiving end of our own wages. What we earned gets washed away. In what? You guessed it. The downpour of his mercy. Instead of death, we get the gift of life, and the greatest tragedy we could ever face is to leave that gift unopened. We need mercy like we need the sun to come up.

No one needs to remind us that we daily fall short. But unfortunately, we have someone whose job it is to do just that. Jesus calls him the "accuser of our brethren" (Revelation 12:9-10 NKJV). An enemy who wants nothing more than for us to believe we're dry souls in the pouring rain. Who tells us we're failures for tripping and therefore unqualified to get back up and continue the race. We have to be careful who we listen to because the only one qualified to hand out judgment hands out mercy instead. And he tells us to keep running.

"Oops!" I reacted to a little year-old girl who fell on the soft grass in front of me during my walk at the park. She seemed unfazed, but her mom didn't miss a beat and said, "Honey, can we please stop running on the grass?" I kept walking and heard her father say, "Let her run. She gets back up. Every time, she gets back up." I could hear the frustrated sigh from the mama bear. "That's why you need to stop running!" she exclaimed as she brushed bits of dirt and grass off her daughter. *Let her run.* I couldn't shake the words of the father. They stuck to me like the grass on the little girl's shirt. Often, when we finally muster the courage to try and then inevitably trip, our own voice pipes up, and we assure ourselves, *See. I knew I couldn't do it.*

It's who we listen to that determines our next step. Will that little girl listen to the voice of her father? Or will she get weighed down by her mother's request? Or maybe she'll let her own fears keep her from getting back up. To state the obvious, it's impossible to never trip. But we must show up imperfectly to the race we're called to run. The only other option is to not show up at all.

"Therefore since we are surrounded by such a great cloud of witnesses, let us throw off everything that hinders and the sin that so easily entangles. And let us run with perseverance the race marked out for us" (Hebrews 12:1 NIV). Listen to the voice of the Father, who cheers you on to persevere: *I know you can't do it perfectly. Just try your best, and I'll wait on the other side of every misstep with mercy to wash the dirt from your knees.* Don't be afraid to fall. Be afraid to never run. His mercy awaits every fall because it's as unstoppable as the sunrise.

A TASTE OF
NEW LIFE

I will give you a new heart, and a new spirit I will put within you. And I will remove the heart of stone from your flesh and give you a heart of flesh.

EZEKIEL 36:26

Making a change doesn't take months; it takes a decision. A life rich in the fruit of love, joy, peace, patience, kindness, goodness, faithfulness, gentleness, and self-control does not grow overnight. You might think, *Wait a minute! You just said making a change doesn't take months.* I think we confuse change with *seeing growth* as a result of that change.

Here in Ezekiel, God tells us he wants to completely change us from the inside out by giving us a brand-new heart. He swaps out the old, and it's in with the new. We'll never be the same after a moment's encounter with our Maker. Our old heart gets uprooted. But just because we get a new root today, that doesn't mean the good fruit will be ready to bite into tomorrow. The change happened, and the growth began immediately. But what does seeing the growth take? You guessed it: Time. Gardens aren't grown in a day, but they can be planted in one.

I think it's safe to say that most of us like to see proof that what we're doing is working. We want affirmation and evidence that we're on the right path. *We want to see the fruit ASAP.* After all, no one sets out to do something hoping it *won't* work. I think the problem is, we can be quick to give up on ourselves when an internal change doesn't result in external growth as fast as we'd like. Chances are, if this is our way of viewing transformation, we also give up on others when we don't witness a fast track to fruitfulness. We might even judge whether they really have committed to change. God is not this way. He's patient. He doesn't get angry at us for not growing fast enough spiritually. He's a great gardener, and even a novice gardener knows you don't dig up the seed just because it hasn't pushed through the dirt yet.

Patience isn't found in the seed; it's found in the gardener. We confuse time with timing. The seed will sprout in its timing. But the farmer must be patient during that time. And even though we're buried deep in the ground, his light still reaches us: "God, being rich in mercy, because of the great love with which he loved us, even when we were dead in our trespasses, made us alive together with Christ—by grace you have been saved" (Ephesians 2:4-5). Don't get discouraged just because you haven't seen fruit yet. Don't forget—you're *alive*. And to be alive is a pretty amazing thing. Just think: All the way back before the beginning of the first garden, God planned to reach us with his light. When there was nothing but darkness, with his breath, he created out of nothing the one thing that would be the source of life in the world. *Let there be light.* And there was light. God created the sun to nourish the ground before there was anything that could grow. So it's not a question of whether we need the light but whether we'll say yes to the rays of salvation.

Don't be afraid you'll never see the fruit. You can't grow overnight. We weren't created that way any more than a seed is. So be patient with others and yourself because that's a part of what God wants to grow in us too. Your dream of having a fruitful life is all in God's timing. Just remember it takes time and requires patience, "and endurance produces character, and character produces hope, and hope does not put us to shame, because God's love has been poured into our hearts through the Holy Spirit who has been given to us" (Romans 5:4-5). Ezekiel reminds us we've been given a new spirit, and Paul reminds us in his letter to the Roman church that the light of God's love enters our hearts through that spirit. Let the light of his love pour in. The seed doesn't will itself to grow. It simply receives the light and comes to life.

A TASTE OF
WISDOM

Those who are wise shall shine like the brightness
of the sky above; and those who turn many to
righteousness, like the stars forever and ever.

DANIEL 12:3

You wouldn't say it's very wise to go on a camping trip and not pack a flashlight. It goes without saying that we need light because it's essential for our survival, especially in the dark of night. We have no ability in ourselves to light the path before our feet any more than we have the ability to hang stars in space. By ourselves, we walk in darkness, or should I say, we stumble around. Because the very purpose of the light itself is to enable us to walk. Without the illumination, we can't move forward without tripping over every rock or getting lost. We underestimate what's needed for a quick walk until the brightness of the sky grows dim.

I love camping with all my heart, but my hands are pretty new to it, which means there's plenty to worry about when it comes to prep. But I'll tell you one thing I don't sweat over even as a beginner: I don't worry about what to bring to face the darkness so I can finish pitching my tent. Why? Because the solution is simple. In fact, it's so straightforward it seems almost excessive to even acknowledge the answer. Before we leave the driveway, we throw the flashlight in the car. Done. Fixed. Was never a problem in the first place.

Even Jesus acknowledged this extremely basic concept: "Are there not twelve hours in the day? If anyone walks in the day, he does not stumble, because he sees the light of this world. But if anyone walks in the night, he stumbles, because the light is not in him" (John 11:9-10). There's only an issue if we don't believe we're headed into the dark, and so we don't come prepared.

"Jesus spoke to them, saying, 'I am the light of the world. Whoever follows me will not walk in darkness, but will have the light of life'" (John 8:12). In his grace, Jesus is saying, *It's not your fault you stumble around in the darkness. You're not the light of the world—that's me. My job is to light the way, and you're invited to simply follow along. I'd love to keep you from stumbling.* Notice what Jesus doesn't say. He doesn't yell at us to pack a flashlight, even though it's obvious we should. Our free will is essential to an intimate relationship with him, so he leaves the choice to us.

Jesus is the light of the world. The light itself is a force to be reckoned with. Once the light is shining, the darkness doesn't have a fighting chance. Light will simply be what it is and do what it does—it shines and drives out darkness. Like a moth to the flame, we come to it not by force but out of a desire for illumination in a dark world. Jesus is not going to pack himself along for our camping trip. He's just going to be the light that he is, and it's up to us to decide if we'll let him shine in our lives.

And when we realize this life is nothing more than a short trip, we recognize we don't have time to waste feeling our way through the dark. If we let the light of the world, Jesus, into our lives, then fear won't rise when the sun sets.

Of course, we can't see in the dark; we're not nocturnal. But the wild thing about choosing to follow Jesus is that he turns around and tells us that we too are the light of the world (Matthew 5:14). That's the point of our trips around the sun: to turn many toward righteousness. To be a light who points others to the Son—the Son of God, Jesus, the light of the world. If we do, we'll enjoy this adventure a whole lot more. We won't worry so much about the bugs or dirt or the rips we'll get in our tent of a body along the way. We'll relax and simply look up at the stars and realize we're one of them. That our work of illumination is eternal, written in the heavens. We'll shine here and now and *forever and ever.*

A TASTE OF
COMMITMENT

*She did not know that it was I who gave her the
grain, the wine, and the oil, and who lavished on
her silver and gold, which they used for Baal.*

HOSEA 2:8

You don't bite into a strawberry expecting to taste an apple. We usually put our expectations behind hopes that are based not on wishful thinking but on assurance. When we expect to taste a sweet berry, we open our mouths with the hope and anticipation of that flavor in mind. The soil of reality is the ground our expectations grow in. We don't want what we hope for to disappoint us; we want to bite into a strawberry and get a strawberry. And a juicy, perfect one at that. But when what we expect and what we get are two different things, our hope is put to shame. We can taste it immediately.

The reality is, all we ever want in this life is found in God's hand. That's a hope we can be sure of. A hope that tethers us to reality so our expectations don't get lost in a fantasy that will do nothing more than leave us high and dry. Because God loves us, he wants to keep our hearts grounded on the certainty of hope.

Any good parent wants the best for their kid. "Which one of you, if his son asks him for bread, will give him a stone? . . . If you then, who are evil, know how to give good gifts to your children, how much more will your Father who is in heaven give good things to those who ask him!" (Matthew 7:9, 11). His protection keeps us from grasping what we think we want.

Imagine reaching through a thorny bush to grab what you *think* is a blackberry, but it's actually poisonous. You might think you're getting a snack, but what you really signed up for is a hospital trip. Unintentionally, but still. That's why we can be glad we have a wise Father who keeps us from getting what we want. Not because he's mean but because he's good. This is what Paul is saying in his letter to Corinth: "'All things are lawful,' but not all things are helpful. 'All things are lawful,' but not all things build up" (1 Corinthians 10:23). You can do anything you want, but not everything is a good idea. In love, God says, "Therefore I will hedge up her way with thorns, and I will build a wall against her, so that she cannot find her paths" (Hosea 2:6). The God who gives Israel grain, wine, and oil is the same God who hedges her in with thorns. He is faithful in both what he gives and what he withholds.

The overarching theme in Hosea (and the whole Bible) is God's faithfulness to an unfaithful bride, the nation of Israel. Over and over, his bride runs off with other lovers. She chooses to lie in bed with other gods. She breaks her covenant with her first love, the one true Creator God. She follows her passions instead of being committed to her vows. And guess how God responds? He stays true to his nature; he responds with faithfulness. Because even "if we are faithless, he remains faithful—for he cannot deny himself" (2 Timothy 2:13). Being faithful is more than something he does. Faithfulness is in God's DNA. Faithful is *who* he is. God will never put our hope to shame. Even when we get what we don't expect from him, he's faithful to give us exactly what we need, whether thorns or grain and wine.

Maybe we have a lot more of God's love to learn about than we think. The opposite of love is not hate—it's indifference. If he didn't love us, he'd let us run off. He wouldn't care. But he cares to the point of thorns; he's jealous for us. May we taste the faithfulness of God's love and never believe we have to go anywhere other than him to find it. We don't need to be afraid. Even in the thorns, we feel the beat of his tender heart. Even when we're a runaway bride, he will be a faithful groom, and what a sweet taste on our lips his commitment is.

A TASTE OF
RESTORATION

*I will restore to you the years that the swarming
locust has eaten, the hopper, the destroyer, and the
cutter, my great army, which I sent among you.*

JOEL 2:25

I f a plume of smoke arises before your eyes, the last thing on your mind is restoration. When our little beach town caught fire, it was hard to watch the army of flames march through our coastal hills. The burn threatened homes as a blanket of haze settled over the coast. Thankfully, when the smoke cleared, no one was hurt, and no homes were lost, but the promise of new life seemed far away as the hills bore their new scars. In the same way, some circumstances can blaze through our lives and leave us wondering, *How will we ever grow from here?*

Whether our decisions have burned us or an unexpected event has left us charred, how are we supposed to expect anything to grow, especially something beautiful, when we're surrounded by ashes?

I'll never forget the hope that rose within me as I drove past those seemingly destroyed, desolate hills and beheld redemption firsthand. The plain shrubs and dried grass that once enveloped the landscape had grown back entirely different. I knew it would never be the same, but I didn't think it would be like this: Beautiful sprawling white flowers covered every inch of the once scorched land. Untamed newness blanketed the ground, wiping out any previous signs of destruction with wildflowers that seemed to reclaim the soil. While watching those blazes burn, it seemed that this lush land would never again be a fertile place, yet the blooms were unstoppable as they reclaimed the singed dirt. Our charming town was now even more picturesque with lush florals instead of withered grass. Beauty for ashes—not just for my eyes to enjoy but for my heart to remember—earth's declaration that new life is never impossible. The wildflowers point our weary souls toward heaven. Their story reveals the heartbeat of our Creator God; he's always in the business of restoration.

I wondered how flowers that had never touched that earth before now completely coated the hillside. With a quick search, I learned wildflowers thrive after a wildfire because the intense heat breaks down the seed coat that otherwise would inhibit their growth. With the temperature turned up, the seed can sprout. The heat doesn't destroy them: It makes them.

It's normal to feel fear when a fire shows up unannounced or, as in the days of Joel, when a devastating swarm of locusts rolls in. It's easy for the ruins around us to drain the hope within. We want the comfort and ease of being led beside quiet waters and green pastures, but in reality, our world is full of heat and pests. It's our nature to avoid and resist pain; our hand is quick to draw back from the hot stove. So when the heat gets turned up, what do we do? It's my hope that where some would see nothing but ashes, we would remember wildflowers are being born.

God redeems not only our situation but also our souls. He's brought us back from the grave with his death, which unearths eternal life for us. God promises to exchange beauty for our ashes. That doesn't mean there won't be fire, but he promises to walk through the flames with us. He turns what's meant for evil and uses it for good. So while we don't live in a world without fire and locusts, we do live in a world with wildflowers. Don't be afraid that God doesn't have a plan for your growth when you find yourself standing in soot, because that's the very ground he has prepared for unparalleled beauty. And if you lit the match yourself, may you have this hope expressed by pastor and author John Mark Comer: "In the aftermath of your sin, when the locusts have left and you're standing in the wreckage of what used to be your life, you could find your hands full of seeds for a new crop, the soil under your toes dark and rich, and maybe even feel a drop of rain on your cheek."* Take heart, little seed, the fire isn't meant to break you but to make you into all God means for you to be.

---

* John Mark Comer, *God Has a Name* (Grand Rapids, MI: Zondervan, 2017), 251.

A TASTE OF
HUNGER

"Behold, the days are coming," declares the Lord GOD, "when
I will send a famine on the land—not a famine of bread,
nor a thirst for water, but of hearing the words of the LORD."

AMOS 8:11

Scripture tells us to think about whatever is true and lovely and to set our minds on things above, not on things below. But what do we do when things here below are making us think about things that are true but not so lovely? How do we take heart when reality wearies our hearts? With daily negative news, natural disasters, hardship, and misfortune, we long to catch a glimpse of the sunset through the fog. And then we read Amos and have to figure out what to do with this: "I will send a famine on the land," God says, "of hearing the words of the LORD." *Great*, you might think.

What if the solution to our hunger for goodness is hidden right there in plain sight? Hearing check: He's not sending a famine *of* the word but of *hearing* the word. The famine is within us, which means the solution likely will be too.

Jesus addressed this hunger in the Sermon on the Mount:

Maybe the solution
to a SATISFIED soul
is to stay hungry.
When we're hungry for
more than the food that
perishes, we'll have an
appetite for the things
that truly NOURISH.

"Blessed are those who hunger and thirst for righteousness, for they shall be satisfied" (Matthew 5:6). The problem is, in Amos's day, the people were not hungry for righteousness. Their hearts weren't open to what God had to say. It's not that God wasn't speaking or wouldn't speak but that they didn't want to listen. God would close their ears because of their already closed hearts. We all know the feeling, perhaps too well, of trying to talk to someone who doesn't want to listen. It's disheartening to try to connect with someone who doesn't want to hit the tennis ball of dialogue back over the net. Conversations can only happen on a two-way street. Otherwise, it's not a conversation but a lecture, and God has no desire to be a dictator; he's a Father. If we're hungry for God, we can come to him and be satisfied, but if we've got no appetite for him, he won't demand we come and sit at the table. So the famine here isn't a lack of food but a lack of a desire to eat in the presence of a Father who won't force-feed.

We can't fill ourselves with a nourishing meal if we spoil our appetite. That's why it's so important for us to figure out what we really want, not what we *think* we want. It sounds like a dream to eat nothing but ice cream, until it isn't. It sounds smart to try to store up money until it leaves you empty in your soul. It feels good to live for the approval of people, until you disappoint them. It feels fun to lay up treasure on earth until a thief breaks in and steals. It sounds enjoyable to live for material things, until they inevitably rust. We usually look through the lens of first-order thinking, which is fast and emotion driven—focused on immediate gratification. But if we pump the brakes and look through the second order of things, we'll receive the wisdom of considering the consequences that follow our behavior. Again, it might sound fun to eat sundaes all day until you consider the ripple effect. We need to look at what we want through the lens of our ultimate desire; otherwise, we'll fill up and still be empty.

Maybe the solution to a satisfied soul is to stay hungry. When we're hungry for more than the food that perishes, we'll have an appetite for the things that truly nourish. The kind of things that don't get stolen, end up lost, or become rusted. Don't fall for the temptation to fill up on something that isn't ultimately fulfilling.

We don't have to be afraid of never being satisfied if we stay hungry and thirsty, because that was at the heart of the promise Jesus spoke to the woman at the well: "Everyone who drinks of this water will be thirsty again, but whoever drinks of the water that I will give him will never be thirsty again" (John 4:13-14). May we never find ourselves in a famine; instead, let's choose to stay hungry for him.

A TASTE OF
HUMILITY

*Though you soar aloft like the eagle, though
your nest is set among the stars, from there I
will bring you down, declares the LORD.*

OBADIAH 1:4

ravity tells us that what goes up must come down. Jesus tells us we must be brought down to be lifted up. Imagine you believed you could fly and gave that idea wings; your meetup with gravity wouldn't exactly be a warm welcome. Gravity is real—enough said. Scripture, like gravity, is absolute truth, and we'll get to know it better either by belief or by experience.

Jesus tells us a truth of the kingdom of heaven that's as real as the law of gravity: "Whoever exalts himself will be humbled, and whoever humbles himself will be exalted" (Matthew 23:12). Pride deceives us by assuring us we can fly high with self-reliant wings, but Jesus confirms that the only thing an empty promise does is set us up for a fall.

Jesus told his disciples, "Apart from me you can do nothing" (John 15:5). Paul later wrote to the Philippians, "I can do all things through him who strengthens me" (Philippians 4:13). These two truths work together. I've learned the hard way that when I try to go anywhere independently from God, I don't make it very far.

When I tried to take care of my body without God's help, I went around in circles. No one sets out to go around the mountain instead of up it. On the inside, I was unsatisfied with the outside, so my goal was to get healthy. My plan was to take control of my food and fitness, but those things quickly took control of me. It's only when I surrendered my health to God that I found it was well with my soul, not because I realized I was enough in myself, but because he became enough for me. I committed to let God lead me in every area of my life after that because I realized it doesn't matter how fast you go if you're going in circles.

Interestingly, commitment seems to make good things great and bad things worse. If we commit to pride, we commit to being brought down. If we commit to humility, we commit to being lifted up in God's timing: "Humble yourselves, therefore, under the mighty hand of God so that at the proper time he may exalt you, casting all your anxieties on him, because he cares for you" (1 Peter 5:6-7). Whether we choose the way of pride or the way of humility, the fruit is a result of the root. Jesus acknowledged this when he said, "A healthy tree cannot bear bad fruit, nor can a diseased tree bear good fruit . . . thus you will recognize them by their fruits" (Matthew 7:18, 20). We will reap what we commit to sow.

When I uprooted the unhealthy root of pride from my health and fitness journey, I enjoyed the sweet fruit that humility produced. God enabled me to take care of my body in a way that brought peace to my soul rather than perfection to the mirror. I found rest instead of stress because I no longer ate or moved to serve myself but did so as acts of simple gratitude for what I've been given: the gift of my body, knitted together by God in my mother's womb.

We'll never be able to do anything perfectly, but God does call us to be good stewards of everything he's given us. From the heart that beats inside our chest, to the money we hold in our hands, to the dreams he's woven into our hearts, may we not commit to steward anything in pride but in faithfulness to the giver. When we realize that everything is a gift from above, we won't get puffed up with pride and then brought down here below.

We are created to soar, but not in our own ability. Pride tempts us to lift ourselves up, but just remember—humility has changed the rules of gravity: The lower we go, the higher we'll fly. So let's stay close to the ground because it's only there we'll find ourselves up in the clouds.

A TASTE OF
JUSTICE

The LORD said, "You pity the plant, for which you did not labor, nor did you make it grow, which came into being in a night and perished in a night. And should not I pity Nineveh, that great city, in which there are more than 120,000 persons who do not know their right hand from their left, and also much cattle?"

JONAH 4:10-11

Perhaps our greatest delights and deepest frustrations are found within the love of God. When someone hurts you deeply, it's a comfort to know you can run into the loving arms of the Father. But you know what really rubs salt into the wound? Watching God be good to the very person who just hurt you. You might embrace the head knowledge that God is slow to anger, but the equality of God's love toward the just and unjust can be hard to wrap your heart around. Do we, like Jonah, throw a temper tantrum when God is kind to our enemies? I'd be lying if I said I never have.

We pray for justice for others, and at the same time, we want God to be merciful toward us. We think it's cool that Jesus stooped down to wash his betrayer's feet until it's our turn to rinse the mud from the person who just kicked that mud at us. Loving your enemy sounds beautiful until you have to wash your own Judas's feet. Then it's not so pretty. It requires proximity when we desire distance. It adds insult to injury when we have to be near them in order to serve them! Proximity alone is hard enough, but combine that with service, and you've got a spoonful of spiritual medicine that is really hard to swallow. And the cherry on top is that you don't even get a tip for your service. (Good thing we just nourished ourselves on a lesson in humility.)

This is exactly the story of Jonah. He didn't want to be the bridge between an unjust people and a just God who happens to be abundantly generous with mercy. As the writer of James says, "Judgment is without mercy to one who has shown no mercy. Mercy triumphs over judgment" (James 2:13). Jonah was so determined to distance himself from the possibility of helping the wicked people of Nineveh that he took a boat in the opposite direction to avoid giving them their foot-washing forgiveness moment. And how did that turn out? Jonah inevitably washed up on the shores of the city that reeked of sin, in need of his own shower. We might get to the end of this story focused on God being merciful to Nineveh and miss how much mercy he spooned out on Jonah.

We withhold mercy from others when we forget the mercy that's been given to us. It seems we have amnesty amnesia, because we're drenched in this mercy every morning, yet even when soaking in it, we don't want to pour a cup of water for someone who's also thirsty for mercy. Freely we have received, and freely we should give. May we remember what we've been given: forgiveness instead of a grudge. Patience instead of anger. Mercy instead of judgment.

We're empowered to treat others how we want to be treated when we remember how God has treated us. His mercy is so all-encompassing that he mentions the cattle when he's talking to Jonah about having pity on the people of the city. The fact that God cares about the cows is the exclamation point to his goodness—if he cares about them, how much more does he care for us, who are made in his image? The ultimate mercy of God is demonstrated through his Son, Jesus, who didn't stop at pouring out water on his enemy's feet but went on to pour out his blood for them at the cross, where justice and mercy meet. God doesn't make us pay for our own sins. In his grace and justice, he settles the bill with his own blood and from his riches of mercy.

We don't need to be afraid of living in poverty, because our debt is paid in the ransom of Jesus. And he didn't just pay so we could no longer be debtors. He paid to make us heirs. Heirs don't work to earn their blessings; they simply receive. Welcome to the kingdom of God: a just land, rich in the soil of mercy, built on the blood of the Lamb, with the door wide open for us all—a place even the cows call home.

A TASTE OF
BEING WITH GOD

He has shown you, O man, what is good; and what
does the LORD require of you but to do justly, to love
mercy, and to walk humbly with your God?

MICAH 6:8 NKJV

The longer I walk with God and the more I come to know him, the more confident I am that we'd all be wise to say "I don't know" more often. I don't know the answer. I don't know the way. But I know the One who does. To walk humbly with God requires within us a willingness to follow, and a follower acknowledges either they don't know the way or there is someone more qualified to lead than them. Jesus doesn't even call himself a leader; he refers to himself as the good shepherd, a shepherd who not only leads his sheep but lays down his very life for them. He invites us to follow him not out of obligation but as an invitation. Our nourishment from Micah reveals what a rich offer this really is.

What does God ultimately want from us? To this, we don't have to answer "I don't know," because God tells us plainly right here in Micah 6. But immediately before he tells us straight up, in verses 6 and 7 he goes down a list of things humans might believe are offerings extravagant enough to be worthy of honoring God. The human brain loves contrast because it helps us understand and conceptualize ideas better. So when God uses contrast here, he's trying to make crystal clear what he requires of us. He begins the list with burnt offerings, thousands of rams, ten thousand rivers of olive oil . . . let's pause right there. Now God is using both contrast and exaggerations. He's being dramatic on the quantity of these potential gifts. Of course he knows it's impossible for us to give him ten thousand rivers of olive oil. That's the point. We can't give what we don't have. He keeps going, and finally, we arrive at the bottom of the list in verse 8. What's there? Not a thousand things of this or a million items of that, but you. And him. Going for a walk.

The only way we're able to do justly and love mercy is if we walk with him. Though he ends on that message, the heart of his heart is to walk with us. David penned this clearly in a psalm: "You will not delight in sacrifice, or I would give it; you will not be pleased with a burnt offering. The sacrifices of God are a broken spirit; a broken and contrite heart, O God, you will not despise" (Psalm 51:16-17). Could it be true? God simply wants *us*?

When Jesus told us he stands at the door of our hearts and knocks (Revelation 3:20), what is he looking to do? Come in and see what he can find? What if he wants nothing more than to come inside? To simply be with us and us be with him? For us to sit with him, like we hear of Mary doing in Luke 10? Unlike her sister, Martha, she is not worrying if everything is perfect, not preoccupied with details of hospitality, and not twisting herself in knots to do everything right. This is a story familiar to many of us, and still, every time I read it, my heart needs the message once again to put my focus on being *with* him rather than doing *for* him.

Mary "walked with" Jesus by resting at his feet. It's not the walk or the sit or the serve that matters, but the *with*. Mary wasn't unfamiliar with helping Martha and serving their guests, and Martha wasn't doing anything bad, but Mary simply chose what was better. Perhaps the greatest thing we can do in this life is simply to give our whole hearts to God.

May we never fret that we have nothing to offer. Simply coming to him is more than enough. The offering in our hand is nothing more than a reflection of our heart, and that is what he loves—when we give him the gift of our hearts. The earth and everything in it are his. May we realize *we* are too. And then simply go for a walk with him.

A TASTE OF
PROTECTION

The LORD is good, a stronghold in the day of trouble;
he knows those who take refuge in him.

NAHUM 1:7

We love before and after photos because we love instant gratification. Wouldn't it be nice to skip over the hard part? Fast-forward through the pain of patience and get right to the happy ending? That may not be realistic, but we can still dream of skipping the flight and effortlessly landing at our destination. My husband doesn't love planes. He gets on board only because he has the end in sight. The hope of touching down motivates him to endure the middle.

I have my own times of impatience. When our kitchen had to be remodeled because of mold, I would have loved a remote control to cut to the finish line. There was no quick fix, and I had no other option but to become the queen of cooking on a camp stove, a crown I initially resisted. And while that's a shallow example, the truth is, we've all faced the deep waters of life and had to tread the ocean of the in-between. The sight of the shore is what gives us the strength to swim. But how do we keep swimming if we feel lost at sea?

We know God promises to give us a future and a hope, so is that where hope is exclusively found, then—in the future? I believe hope is both the rope we hold onto for tomorrow and the anchor that holds us for today. It seems the author of Hebrews confirms this idea as we are encouraged to "hold fast to the hope *set before us.* We have this as a sure and steadfast *anchor* of the soul" (Hebrews 6:18-19, emphasis mine). Hope is both before us and with us. God sent Nahum, whose name means "comfort," into the most hopeless time of Judah's history up until that point. To give comfort is to extend hope and strength to another. When I want to build a discouraged friend's hope, I speak encouraging words they can receive to fill up their reserves. In the people of Judah, God sensed hearts void of hope, so he sends them hope with a beating heart. When they heard, "Hi, my name is Nahum," their spirits heard, "Hi, my name is hope." Perhaps hope is found where we are because of someone who is with us.

There was a time when my soul experienced the dark belief that there was no light at the end of the tunnel. I desperately wanted a glimpse of hope so I could have the strength to carry on. I tried to see; the light seemed nowhere to be found. I felt like I didn't have the strength to carry on, so my only hope was to let go, even though that didn't feel like a very hopeful thing to do. I'll forever be grateful that what I found at the end of my rope was someone who found me. I thought I needed my own strength to carry on;

I didn't realize until I let go that I was actually being carried. Hope met me. Not because it finally showed up but because I finally had eyes to see God was there all along. The light wasn't at the end of the tunnel; he was with me every step of the way, including at the end of my rope.

May we realize our Savior is with us always, not just when we need to be rescued. The lifeguard is always on duty, but sometimes we only remember he's there when the waves rise. After a full day of teaching by the sea, Jesus invited his disciples to hop in the boat with him: "Let us go across to the other side" (Mark 4:35). When the wind stirred up the sea and dumped rising waves into their boat, the disciples were shocked to see Jesus getting some shut-eye. In their moment of hopelessness, they forgot the promise found within Jesus's initial invitation: "Let us go across." When the waves rise, fear will rise too, but we can hold on to the hope that's gone before us (he already told us we're going to make it to the other side) so we don't despair that the hope beside us is asleep. Hope is unearthed in the promise itself, so let's follow Jesus and be grounded right in the middle of the storm, because the guarantee is sure: We'll soon be on solid ground again.

A TASTE OF
FRUITFULNESS

*Though the fig tree should not blossom, nor fruit be on
the vines, the produce of the olive fail and the fields
yield no food, the flock be cut off from the fold and
there be no herd in the stalls, yet I will rejoice in the
LORD; I will take joy in the God of my salvation.*

HABAKKUK 3:17-18

Let's leave behind a shallow, get-your-toes-wet, circumstantial kind of faith and experience the joy of a "jump in so deep you discover an ocean in the middle of the desert" kind of faith. A faith that gets its hair wet and doesn't care if it dries frizzy. The kind of faith that grows the impossible, is rooted deep in love, never gives up hope, and sees the unfruitful trees yet still finds a reason to sing.

Desperate times call for deep faith. Jesus told a parable about a sower going out to scatter seed—a metaphor for the Word of God. The seeds land on different soil—a metaphor for the readiness of those who hear the Word. The goal of growth is uprooted when the seeds land on rocky or thorny soil, are snatched up by hungry birds, or are withered by a scorching sun. I remember being young

Whether circumstances are GOOD or BAD, it doesn't matter because our faith is not in what's happening AROUND us but in who is ABOVE us.

in my faith, and someone read off statistics about how many souls will walk away from their faith as they get older. The moment felt strangely reminiscent of when the disciples gathered around the table for their final meal with Jesus before the cross and heard the shocking news that one of them would betray him. Like the disciples, I wondered, *Is it I, Lord?*

The thought of falling away and leaving Jesus behind was bone chilling. I don't share that to show you my perfect faith—we're all still being refined—but at the heart of pure faith is simply a heart that receives Jesus with no reservations. Faith that says, *I will follow no matter what.*

At the end of the sower and seed parable, Jesus explains the good soil—the ready heart—plainly as "the ones who hear the word and accept it" (Mark 4:20). Well, Paul writes in his letter to Corinth, "So faith comes from hearing, and hearing through the word of Christ" (Romans 10:17). Jesus doesn't say the soil is "perfect"; he says the soil accepts the seed. Perhaps it's not that the good soil never has any hungry birds fly over or isn't under the same hot sun but that it receives the seed and protects it whatever comes its way. Faith is not a matter of circumstance but choice. It seems then that good soil is good because it doesn't let outside or inside obstacles determine its fate; it simply says yes to the seed.

Strong faith is usually thought of as tenacious and perseverant. I'd say it is also adaptable and flexible. It can rejoice always. It can be fruitful anywhere. We're strong when our faith isn't dependent on our conditions but on our Creator. So whether circumstances are good or bad, it doesn't matter because our faith is not in what's happening around us but in who is above us. The secret to growing a truly thriving faith in difficult times is realizing that God goes beyond giving our hearts strength on hard days. He puts a song in our mouths for starless nights. Like the psalmist wrote, "The LORD is my strength and my song; he has become my salvation" (Psalm 118:14). He is both what we need to face the day and the one we can rejoice in during it.

He's become our salvation. He puts breath in our lungs and then places a melody there too. God saves our souls and goes on to fortify them too. He makes us so resilient to hard days, we can face them not only with strength but also with *joy.* That's God's saving grace in our life: We put our faith in who he is, and he does more than make us well—he makes us flourish. Think about it. Six times in the gospels we hear this classic line: "Your faith has made you well." Salvation is rooted in the same word as salve, but the wild thing is the people Jesus healed didn't leave just feeling well—they leapt and sang because one touch from their Savior filled them with uncontainable joy; it spilled out of their souls for everyone to see and hear. And what's required for this? Nothing more than a receptive heart, because even pavement has the potential to be fertile ground. When you spot a flower pushing its way through the sidewalk and reaching toward the sky, may it be a reminder that faith can be found anywhere.

A TASTE OF
GLADNESS

*The LORD your God is in your midst, a mighty one who will
save; he will rejoice over you with gladness; he will quiet
you by his love; he will exult over you with loud singing.*

ZEPHANIAH 3:17

T hinking about God loudly singing over me is hard to picture.
Not because it's not amazing but because it's *so* amazing. I
mean *God* singing over *me*? One of the theories behind why
humor works is that we find humor in the incongruity between
our expectations and reality. Two fundamentally incompatible con-
cepts come together in a way that makes us expect one thing but
experience another, essentially making us laugh at our own disappointed expectations.

Imagine the expectations-versus-reality posts you see online that
are so hilarious because they're unharmonious. Some of us think
of God mainly as David as he wondered, "What is man that you
are mindful of him, and the son of man that you care for him?"
(Psalm 8:4). Then consider the juxtaposition of God belting out
a melody over us. That's the unharmonious hilarity I feel—that

feeling of surprise that God isn't just "up there," mindful of us, but he's also down here, singing over us.

Bring this wild scenario down to earth for a minute. Imagine the president of the United States dancing down the street in front of you. The reality is, we roll our eyes at the thought of that because our expectation of someone in that position doing that seems so out of character. That's how I feel when I reflect on these words in Zephaniah. It casts God in a light where his divinity looks a lot more "human" than we might think. When we picture this scene of intimate connection with the Creator of all, the King of kings, the Lord of lords, singing over someone, we can't escape that it requires great affection and vulnerability.

I'm willing to be vulnerable and sing on a drive with my husband, but the list of my audience beyond him is pretty short. However, when I am in the car alone with the music on, you know I'm belting out a song at the top of my lungs and calling it "singing." We sing with unrestrained abandon when we feel safe. There's no one there to judge us, so the open road or even the shower invites us to relax into who we really are and sing. On pitch or not. (For me . . . not.)

Maybe nothing is new under the sun because King David seemed to feel this when he danced in the street: "As the ark of the LORD came into the city of David, Michal the daughter of Saul looked out of the window and saw King David leaping and dancing before the LORD, and she despised him in her heart" (2 Samuel 6:16). What royalty "should" do gets shattered in the best possible way here.

We put a song in the mouth of God. This scripture is something to savor, like hard candy. It is something we shouldn't hurry through but let dissolve in our soul and shape our view of God in the most picturesque way: He can't contain how he feels about us, so he lets it spill out through physical expression. His joy is a cup of melodies that overflows into our ears. And think about it: What's the purpose of a song? To make the listener hear the beat of the tune and of the songwriter's heart. God is saying, "My heart beats for yours." How could we not love him for that? As John says, "We love because he first loved us" (1 John 4:19). May God's authenticity with us invite us to be authentic before him. May his love become as real to our soul, as a song is to our ears. May the sound waves be not just something we hear but something that makes us reach to turn up the volume so we can be immersed as we listen. May his love be so loud in our lives that we feel it reverberate through our cells. Like our favorite song that gives us no choice but to sing along, may he be our favorite tune. And maybe we'll find, like David, that we just can't help but dance along.

A TASTE OF
PRIORITIES

You looked for much, and behold, it came to little. And
when you brought it home, I blew it away. Why? Declares
the LORD of hosts. Because of my house that lies in ruins,
while each of you busies himself with his own house.

HAGGAI 1:9

Our life is the sum of our priorities. We make time for the things we value, and we make excuses for things we don't. The reality of that statement can be sobering because it requires us to take responsibility for our choices. The redemption of that statement is freeing because it allows us to clearly see what matters most to us. Picture it—a life without priorities doesn't look very promising. We prove to ourselves and the people around us where our hearts lie with how we spend our time. Of course, everyone wants to spend time well, but it seems we can struggle to do just that.

When we prioritize the temporary over the eternal, we find within us a hollowness inside our souls. There's something that stirs wonder in my heart hearing about famous people with hearts after God—the person who has "everything" possessing the one thing everyone needs. It reminds me of when a wealthy young man came to Jesus and asked him what he must do to receive eternal life. Jesus answered him that he already knew the commandments and proceeded to list some of them: "Do not commit adultery, do not murder, do not steal, do not bear false witness, honor your father and mother" (Luke 18:20). The rich man confirmed he'd done these things since youth. Jesus responded to that with "You still lack one thing. Sell everything you have and give to the poor, and you will have treasure in heaven. Then come, follow me" (Luke 18:22 NIV). Jesus taps into the number one priority in this guy's heart and then instructs him to get rid of it. All. Of. It. Jesus is guiding him to make room. Room for what exactly? Notice one of the commandments Jesus just so happens to *not* list at the beginning of their conversation is the *most* important one. It seems Jesus tries to indirectly reveal this by putting his finger directly on the one thing that mattered most to him, a hint that the one thing he lacked was the fulfillment of the greatest commandment of all: to love God with all your heart. *All.* That's what matters the most.

Jesus invites him to rearrange his list in proper order to sell all he has, give it to the poor, and then follow him. The young guy gets really sad because as sincere as he was, he was also quite wealthy. You get the picture. Jesus was setting his priorities straight; before he called him to follow him, he desired him to love him with everything he had. That's what Jesus wanted more than anything: the top spot in his heart.

Every time I've tried to prioritize anything over my love for God, it's brought me sadness. It wasn't as though my life necessarily crashed and burned (probably because of God's mercy), but the river of life that ran through me felt shallow. Whether it was boys, my body, or my business, it didn't matter what was at the top; if it wasn't Jesus, it always seemed to bring me down. I must regularly ask God to search my heart and be the king of my heart because only then can everything else be life-giving.

May we make God the priority of our life because he gave his life for us. We don't need to be afraid we'll lack anything if we seek him first because he promised to give us everything if we do that one thing. When lesser things make their way to the top of our lists, God doesn't write us off as a failure. He simply invites us to rearrange our list. Whatever the deepest dream your heart holds, if you delight in him the most, you'll find every desire fulfilled. Don't take my word for it—check out Psalm 37:4. If we lack *the one* thing, we'll live without life, but what a treasure to know the list of things that really matter isn't very long. May we make room to love God with everything we are and find he fits the space so well, we don't want even one more thing.

ZECHARIAH

A TASTE OF
SATISFACTION

Say to them, Thus declares the LORD of hosts:
Return to me, says the LORD of hosts, and I will
return to you, says the LORD of hosts.

ZECHARIAH 1:3

There's nothing like a refreshing sip of cold water in the middle of an intense workout. But that drink isn't possible unless I have held my thermos under running water before I got to work; it must be filled up to pour out. The same is true for our lives spiritually—but how are we practically to return to God and be filled up? Maybe the answer is found right in the middle of our example: *We stay thirsty.*

There are a couple of different kinds of thirst in my life. I don't thirst for my morning coffee the same way I thirst for a drink of water during a sweaty workout. One of them I want and one of them I need. I imagine God wants to be considered both. As the psalmist wrote, "As a deer pants for flowing streams, so pants my soul for you, O God" (Psalm 42:1). But God also tells us, "You will seek me and find me, when you seek me with all your heart" (Jeremiah 29:13). Of course, we *need* God, but God wants us to also

127

want him. And here, we catch a glimpse of the relational aspect of God's heart. He says, *If you do this, then I'll do this.* There's a back and forth. A give and take. Because that's what you do in a relationship—you relate to one another. Relationships depend on this, it's their lifeblood. If the give-and-take stops, the relationship dies.

My mom used to tell me it's like a tennis match. If you don't hit the ball back, the game is over. Even if you don't make it over the net each time or play perfectly, the point is to show the other person you're in the game. You hit, and they hit back. It's the same way with God. We see the concept of if/then throughout the entirety of Scripture. All the way back in Genesis, God tells Abraham, "Go from your country.... And I will bless you" (Genesis 12:1-2), and even if you fast-forward to Revelation, Jesus says, "I stand at the door and knock. If anyone hears my voice and opens the door, I will come in to him and eat with him" (Revelation 3:20). You do this, and I'll do that. There's interaction, and it's never one-sided because God desires a real, true, and deep relationship with us, and that can only happen if both parties regularly engage with each other.

If you got all that, then prepare for a plot twist. A little verse comes along that kind of blows up the whole thing in the best way: "If we are faithless, he remains faithful—for he cannot deny himself " (2 Timothy 2:13). There's a rock-solid constant about God: He remains unchanging in his character. He will be faithful because that's *who* he is. If you don't hold up your side of the relationship, he still will. He will go after us when we get lost. If we decide to willingly leave, he won't force us to stay. However, he will be there when we come back. He is true to himself and will always be who and what he is: *faithful.*

May we come to him daily because he'll faithfully be there. We come to him on our favorite spot on the couch with warm coffee in hand. Because when we do that, we find ourselves not on a couch but at the feet of Jesus. We come to him as we take a sip of water during our run along the beach, watching the golden rays of the sun wave the day good-bye. Because when we do that, we find ourselves not running on the shore but being carried by the truth that his thoughts for us outnumber the grains of sand. We return to him, not in place but in heart. May we come to him again and again and find he satisfies our panting soul even as we wake up thirsty the next day for more of him.

A TASTE OF
ATTENTIVENESS

*Then those who feared the LORD spoke with one
another. The LORD paid attention and heard them,
and a book of remembrance was written before him of
those who feared the LORD and esteemed his name.*

MALACHI 3:16

We take note of the things we want to remember. We note the particular blue of someone's eyes or the sound of their laugh—you don't just look at the person; you take notice of them. Something stays in your mind about their presence. You carry that memorable trait or encounter in your heart because in some way, it's made an impression, and you take mental notes because a part of you wants to remember it. Of all the things I've noted in the Scriptures, this particular moment in Malachi stands out because God not only tells us he keeps a journal but reveals what he writes about. It seems remarkable that we are allowed to peek into the mind of God and know what he jots down to remember. He doesn't keep it a mystery. He swings the door wide open to reveal that his attention lies with us.

The psalmist put it like this: "Because he bends down to listen,

I will pray as long as I have breath!" (Psalm 116:2 NLT). God, who formed the clouds and made them dust beneath his feet, bends down to us not only because he wants to hear but because he wants to *listen*. He takes it one step further to note it so it will never be forgotten. He doesn't write it down in secret but makes the secrets of his heart known. To us. God lets us in. When we bring him into our conversations, our words are something he wants to cherish forever. Our words hold meaning, a peek behind the curtain of our hearts.

As Jesus described it, "The good person out of the good treasure of his heart produces good, and the evil person out of his evil treasure produces evil, for out of the abundance of the heart his mouth speaks" (Luke 6:45). Could God be revealing that what he takes note of when we talk about him is whether our hearts treasure him?

My husband recently mentioned a conversation he had with someone who told him about a well-known athlete who is a follower of Jesus. The friend watched first out of interest in the sport but then took notice because of who the athlete *was*. The well-known person's heart was noteworthy in the same way our heart is noteworthy to God. It made me think about my favorite local bakery where the most delicious gluten-free peach scone in existence awaits my lips. (If you are around me long you realize many things remind me of food or food stories. Trust me, this relates. I promise.) When I recently went to the counter to buy it, the girl who wrapped my treat made mention of God, which made me take note of her. I think this is what God does with us.

When you and I talk about God, he notices our heart for him. Our conversations are amplified in the Creator's ear. When we talk about him, God pays attention. Why? Because our words reveal what matters enough to our hearts to bring it to our lips, and God can't help but savor every last syllable.

May we never withhold our prayers out of fear that he doesn't hear. He not only opens his ears but also bends down and opens his hands to respond to our request, if only we should ask. Perhaps the most damaging lie we could ever believe is that God hears us but doesn't listen. Think about what someone does after you finish talking and they're done listening. They *respond*. Whether with words or tears or maybe an embrace, their response tells you they care. Don't ever forget or doubt that God cares so much about you he is ready to write down what you say about him, and he cares so deeply, he will respond.

We were once a dream in the heart of God, so how could we not share our dreams with him? If we pay attention, we might hear the marks of his pen and realize he's always paying attention to us.

NEW TESTAMENT

Whether you leap into Matthew or take one step at a time into Revelation, let's take with us a desire to taste and see with new eyes the beauty of the old rugged cross, and with a hungry heart to be satisfied by Jesus's abundant love. To feel the warmth of Scripture bring our souls back to life—to be nourished by truth so we can flourish.

A TASTE OF
BELONGING

*Behold, a voice from heaven said, "This is my
beloved Son, with whom I am well pleased."*

MATTHEW 3:17

E ven if it's been a while since you've heard his voice, God has never stopped speaking to you. Have you ever found it hard to hear him through all the noise constantly pouring in? For years, I searched for his assuring voice in everything from my own performance, the mirror, other people's opinions, and even relationships. Because of that off-track pursuit, I went in circles trying to reach a goalpost that seemed to move as soon as I got close. It had been so long since I heard the voice of truth that when I finally did, it was difficult to believe him because the lies were deeply rooted within my soul.

Everything else I gave ear to called me by a different name. My performance called me unproven, the mirror called me not good enough, other people called me unworthy, and certain relationships called me by name only to leave me. I was confused; I didn't even know who *Cambria* was anymore. It was at this lowest point in my life when I heard God's voice break through the darkness that surrounded me and the chains that bound me. I recognized the voice of my Father because he called me "daughter."

God set me free and began a process of redemption, healing, and being nourished by truth, something I could never have imagined was possible. This is exactly what the Spirit does: He brings freedom. By the power of the Spirit, we realize everything we're looking for is found in him. We find rest in him because our worth becomes unhitched from our performance, appearance, and the opinions of others or even ourselves. We can rest inside a worth no longer dependent upon anything outside of God.

This worth is an inherent value tied not to what we do but to who we are to God. Look at what the Father says even before Jesus did anything that caused people to think, *Hey, he must be the Son of God!* "This is my beloved Son, with whom I am well pleased" (Matthew 3:17). The Father is pleased with his Son simply because he's his. We'll only try to prove our worth if we look for it outside of him. Jesus faced a challenge to this belief when, immediately after the Father calls him "beloved Son," the Spirit drives him into the wilderness to be tempted: "And the tempter came and said to him, 'If you are the Son of God, command these stones to become loaves of bread'" (Matthew 4:3). There was no question in the devil's mind that Jesus was the Son of God. He wasn't using "if" here as if he didn't know who he was dealing with; he was only trying to get Jesus to prove his identity by *doing* rather than *being*. Jesus didn't fight back with proof but fell back into truth. He knew who he was because he knew *whose* he was, and may the same be true for us.

There's an enemy of our souls who wants nothing more than to deceive us too. The devil went on from challenging Jesus on *who* he was, to how much *truth* he knew, to whether he *believed* in the truth or not. This part of Jesus's life is our example of how to overcome our adversary; we, too, can trust who we are by knowing whose we are and what he says and then live by every word that comes from his mouth, believing it to be true. We are daily in a fight to rest in who we are to God. In order to do that, we need to know his Word and believe it as truth. Only then will we be able to resist the lies and stand firm. If we build an identity based on works or our self-perceived worth, we'll soon find ourselves looking through a cracked mirror. But if we set the mirror down and see ourselves through the eyes of the Father who sent his Son to bring us into the family of God, we'll realize our search for worth ends at the cross. If you listen closely, you'll realize he's never once stopped calling out your name.

If we build an identity based on WORKS or our self-perceived WORTH, we'll soon find ourselves looking through a CRACKED MIRROR.

A TASTE OF
BALANCE

*Jesus withdrew with his disciples to the sea, and a
great crowd followed, from Galilee and Judea . . .
And he told his disciples to have a boat ready for
him because of the crowd, lest they crush him.*

MARK 3:7,9

We live in a culture of consumerism and achievement where "more" equals better. Go faster. Hustle harder. Get more done. Hurry. Work your fingers to the bone. Rise 'n' grind. Maybe you've even said these to yourself to try to accomplish more.

Busy is no longer the way we live but someone we've become. Don't get me wrong, I love being productive. Time well spent is fulfilling, but productivity becomes problematic when it becomes a measure of worth. When we work to prove our worth, it will suck us dry. But when we work from our worth, we'll be a wellspring for others, not burnt out and dried up but overflowing.

There's an idea floating around that Jesus didn't have boundaries, based on the fact that he gave his life for us—as if his giving of his life for us means he never set limits. The Jesus I read about in the Gospels is not this way. He knew his value came from the Father alone, and he set forth to do the will of the Father by *creating limits* in his life. The busier Jesus got, the more he would retreat to be alone on a mountain with his Father (Mark 1:35). He regularly walked and sat by the beach alone and even invited his disciples to come away by themselves to a desolate place to find rest (Mark 6:31). Jesus did not busy himself to fulfill expectations of others but came only to do the will of the Father.

When Jesus was a twelve-year-old child, his parents left Jerusalem to go back home after Passover. They didn't realize their child wasn't in the caravan until after they had traveled an entire day. After three long days of searching for him back in Jerusalem, they found Jesus sitting in the temple. When his worried mama told him they'd been anxiously looking for him, Jesus's response is a bit shocking. He didn't put his head down and say, "Sorry, Mom." He had the audacity to question his parents: "Why were you looking for me? Did you not know that I must be in my Father's house?" (Luke 2:49). Jesus was a people-person but didn't live to please people. He even said, "Blessed is the one who is not offended by me" (Matthew 11:6).

Jesus was never hurried by the demands of others, even the ones he closely knew and deeply loved. Even when his friend Lazarus was dying, he didn't drop everything, pick up his pace, and sprint to heal him: "Now Jesus loved Martha and her sister and Lazarus. So, when he heard that Lazarus was ill, he stayed two days longer in the place where he was" (John 11:5-6). If you're like me, you'll read that and at first think, *Well if Jesus loved them, he would hurry to make it in time to heal his friend!* But the reality is Jesus *did* love them. This truth is still a hard pill for me to swallow. Just because you love someone doesn't mean you will never disappoint them.

Because Jesus knew who he was, he had an interruptible, unhurried, unrushed presence about him, always. He was regularly misunderstood by people and still loved them at the same time. We are to give, love, and serve the people in our lives out of a place of rest. We aren't to live for the approval of people and their every expectation of us, because if we try, it will be like trying to serve two masters. Jesus had no limits to his love but without question had limits to what he committed himself to do. By the way, Jesus arrived after Lazarus had died . . . and he raised him from the dead. Lazarus got more than a healing; he got a resurrection.

Jesus was productive because he was able to both work and rest from a place of assurance; he knew where he came from and where he was going. So whether he was "busy" on a mountain, taking a nap, giving sight to the blind, or barbecuing on the beach for his disciples, he never once preoccupied himself trying to prove himself by pleasing others or feeling undeserving of rest. May we busy ourselves resting in the truth that sets us free from the need to do more . . . and discover the only kind of "more" that's better is more of him.

A TASTE OF
POSSIBILITY

*When Jesus heard these things, he marveled at him,
and turning to the crowd that followed him, said, "I
tell you, not even in Israel have I found such faith."*

LUKE 7:9

When a problem makes us feel powerless, hope has a way of slipping through our fingertips, because our logical minds have a hard time agreeing with faith. Before trouble comes, we more easily embrace unseen faith. We're more willing to say wholeheartedly that we trust beyond a doubt. But when we can't see beyond the step we're on and hit rocky ground, the doubts come. *How can I know for certain I won't slip if I can't see the way in front of me?*

Walking by faith sounds nice until we're weighed down by disbelief because it seems more logical, more real, than faith. Maybe we even consider it wise of us to look at a situation and laugh because the thought of anything ever changing feels beyond hopeless. We're smart to be skeptical, right? Wait. Let's be more faithful than doubtful. If we're asking, *How is this going to be possible?*

it's time to pause and ask the real question that leads to a very real answer we can stand on: *What if nothing is too hard for God?*

There are two times in Scripture we read that Jesus marveled. First, in the Gospel of Mark in Jesus's hometown of Nazareth, the people in the synagogue listened to Jesus and were amazed by his wisdom and words. They could not believe him. Literally. The carpenter's son? No one would have dared to believe that Jesus, whom they watched grow up, could somehow be the Son of God. Impossible. Or so it seemed according to them. So Jesus could do no mighty works there. Their lack of faith left no room for miracles at the table. Jesus marveled. Sadly, his awe was at the people's *unbelief.*

Just north of there in the town of Capernaum, a centurion's servant was dying. This military officer wasn't at church listening to a sermon but was busy working for the Romans. He had only heard of who Jesus was. In desperation, he pleaded with Jesus to come and heal his sickly servant before death knocked at the door. As Jesus drew near, suddenly, the centurion had a change of heart. He realized that Jesus didn't need to place his hands on the servant; instead, the centurion needed to place his faith in the hands of the Healer. He simply asked Jesus, "Say the word, and let my servant be healed" (Luke 7:7). Jesus marveled because this man's faith went beyond logical understanding. His faith was quite literally a stretch.

It boils down to this: Those who had every reason to believe chose not to, and those who had no hope left dared to believe. One didn't believe a word Jesus said, and another's faith hung on every word. Imagine that. Our faith invites the hand of God to move mountains in our lives. Some might think it's impossible that we can somehow influence what God does. But that's exactly what faith does. It rises above our circumstances to meet God, who has the power, with just a word, to shift the course of our lives.

Keep in mind that there are 86,400 seconds in a day, and all it takes is one prayer in one of those seconds for everything to change. It doesn't take a lot of faith for things to change; you just need to put what little faith you do have in the hands of the One who does exceedingly more.

When your faith is buried under fear, may God grow a garden from your grave. When your dream is at a dead end, may God turn the wall of water into a walkway. May your hope be resurrected in the hands of the One who brought your very soul back to life. If he can do that, what can't he do? May we, too, marvel that the answer to the question "Is anything too hard for God?" is "Nothing." And what a thing to smile about.

A TASTE OF
BEING KNOWN

*I am the good shepherd. I know my
own and my own know me.*

JOHN 10:14

I stood on the edge of a cliff overlooking the water while my husband surfed the last light of the day. There's nothing like the golden hour. The sun-dripped coastline is magical, heavenly. I decided to take a short walk along the sea cliff with our little dog to get to one of my favorite lookouts. I gazed down from above the water to see all the surfers sprinkled throughout the lineup and tried to spot which one was mine. With all of them in wet suits and the strong sun glare, I thought, *How am I going to know which one is Bo?*

Then I spotted him. I knew for certain. Not because I could see his face but because I knew his paddle. I just knew. You know how you can hear someone in your family walk through your house, and you recognize the person by the sound of their footsteps? You just *know*.

Once I knew I was looking at him, I could tell he was looking for me. No doubt he wondered if I was still there. Sometimes in our faith, we find ourselves out there too, paddling back and forth and looking around for God, wondering if he is even there anymore. Is he really with us? Does he really know what I'm going through? It can be hard to believe that he's with us because we're not yet face-to-face, but may we always remember and know with certainty that even though we don't see him, he's never lost sight of us.

God more than sees us, he *intimately* knows us. He knows our paddle out in the water and how we walk down the hall. As the psalmist declared, "You know when I sit down and when I rise up; you discern my thoughts from afar" (Psalm 139:2). Down to the hairs on your head, you're fully seen and deeply known.

But it doesn't stop there. It says his own know him as he knows us. Do you feel like you intimately know God? We are *all* invited to answer that question. That's the key: invited. Think about that: We are invited to intimately know God in a way that we know the sound of his voice and the way he moves in our lives. Then we're invited to get lost inside his heart and simultaneously find ourselves there.

How can it be possible to really know the One who says, "For as the heavens are higher than the earth, so are my ways higher than your ways and my thoughts than your thoughts" (Isaiah 55:9)? That reads like distance—a set-apartness that is hard to bridge, right? The good news—the best news—is that it doesn't stop there. We also read this promise: "You will seek me and find me, when you seek me with all your heart" (Jeremiah 29:13). This might be the most interesting thing about God: He can be entirely unsearchable *and* completely known. God is very much "both/and." He's not one or the other; he is one and the same. He is both the lion and the lamb, the servant and the king, divine and human, the beginning and the end, the first and the last. The list goes on and on. To know God is to constantly pull him out of the box we try to put him in and then let him invite us back into his heart, where a familiar road regularly winds into the unknown.

May we take the time to get to know God. May our hearts fall in love with his. May he show us his character plainly and simultaneously invite us to search out his nature in the depths of the ocean that is Scripture. We don't ever have to be afraid that he won't be found. There will just simply be more of him to know. May we hear his familiar footsteps approach the door of our heart and then open the door with curiosity in our soul . . . *I know him. What will he show me today?*

A TASTE OF
GUIDANCE

*They went through the region of Phrygia and Galatia, having
been forbidden by the Holy Spirit to speak the word in Asia.
And when they had come up to Mysia, they attempted to go
into Bithynia, but the Spirit of Jesus did not allow them.*

ACTS 16:6-7

The hope of being led by God's Spirit to do his will in our
individual lives is held out to us right here. Paul and his fellow workers traveled to spread the gospel throughout the
world, and on one particular spot during their journey, they head
toward a certain region, but the Holy Spirit does not permit them
to go. Then they head somewhere else, and the same thing happens: The Spirit of Jesus does not allow them to go. Acts 16 then
tells us they depart again, and in the middle of the night, a vision
comes to them, and they receive clear direction from God. So what
do we see here? God's people being led specifically by his Spirit,
down to the very step. We see the proverb come to life: "The heart
of man plans his way, but the LORD establishes his steps" (Proverbs 16:9). God cares enough to lead us in every detail of our lives.

At the core of our hearts, we desire to do God's will, and we can be assured he'll lead us, but sometimes we aren't sure what that looks like in our lives. And what if we'd rather be led in paths of convenience than paths of righteousness? Well, we can thank God for giving us the Holy Spirit, also called the Helper, who will lead us and guide us into all truth. This means we should, as children of God, regularly expect his Spirit to lead us. As Paul wrote, "For all who are led by the Spirit of God are sons of God" (Romans 8:14). To not believe you'll be led by God in your life is *to believe* in an estranged sort of god who's divorced from Scripture. Even Jesus experienced the Spirit's leading in his own life. You might think, *Well yeah, that's Jesus.* But in the book of Acts, we see the Spirit works the same way in Jesus's followers as the Spirit worked in him. So it's no longer a question of *if* the Spirit wants to lead us but *how*.

Our clue is reading "Spirit said" over and over in Scripture. However, some logical questions flood our brains: How? Is that an audible sound? An impression? A feeling? The Bible doesn't explicitly say. We might conclude the way God communicates to his children is almost as unique as his children themselves. I don't talk to my baby niece the way I talk to my adult sister. It's understandable that we long to be told a clear way to hear from the Spirit, receive straightforward instructions about what he sounds like, and be given the inside scoop about what he's going to say. But communication of the Spirit is more ethereal and takes more relational involvement. The Bible doesn't say something about every single situation in your life, but there are principles, truths, and spiritual wisdom for everything we will encounter. Practically, teaching precedes leading. The Spirit will guide us into truth and bring to remembrance the Word of God for us. So if we want to be led by the Spirit, we must have deep interaction with the Word.

Talk to God, stay in his Word, and his Spirit that lives within you *will* lead you. As mysterious as it is, we don't have to be afraid. He will make it known. It might be through a whisper, the wind, a dream, a specific scripture, a word from a friend, or through the open and closed doors along your path. Would we prefer a concrete plan spelled out? Probably. But we'd miss the adventure that comes with the Spirit being like the wind. In my life, I remember being saddened when I moved to a new town when I was younger, but if God didn't move my family, I wouldn't have started my YouTube channel, which means I wouldn't be writing this to you today. God's Spirit has spoken to me through his Word, whispered a promise to my heart through the wind, and prompted me to go to certain places that opened specific doors. Albert Einstein is often quoted as saying, "Coincidence is God remaining anonymous," but may we see his Spirit even when he doesn't sign his name. Open your ears and you may discover he'll take your heart places your mind could never imagine. And maybe that's exactly how it's supposed to be.

A TASTE OF
PRESENCE

*I am sure that neither death nor life, nor angels nor rulers,
nor things present nor things to come, nor powers, nor height
nor depth, nor anything else in all creation, will be able to
separate us from the love of God in Christ Jesus our Lord.*

ROMANS 8:38-39

Our search for God has nothing to do with location; it's about awareness of his presence. No matter where we are, he is there. He carries our hearts with him no matter where our feet find themselves. The mystery is, we carry him too. Jesus's last words to his disciples before he ascended to be at the right hand of the Father were "And behold, I am with you always, to the end of the age" (Matthew 28:20). Right before Jesus left, he promised always to be with us. It seems you wouldn't say "I'll never leave you" and then, well, leave. But listen to his assurance: "Nevertheless, I tell you the truth: it is to your advantage that I go away, for if I do not go away, the Helper will not come to you. But if I go, I will send him to you" (John 16:7). The Helper—Jesus's reference to the Holy Spirit—reveals God doesn't primarily live inside walls but inside hearts. We know God is always with us, but we seem to forget that he wants us to be with him. God's presence is always present, but are we present with him?

A person's presence feels almost indulgent in such a distracted world. Nothing fills the heart like being the recipient of undivided attention. And there's nothing quite as disheartening as when someone is with you, but they're not truly there with you. They might be next to you, but their heart and thoughts are far away. When you hang out with someone, you want all of them; you want their presence to be present with you. You want them to look at you and listen to you and be immersed in you and what you're saying. And vice versa.

I imagine God feels the same. He gives us his undivided attention every waking moment of our lives. He is there when we're on a long drive to nowhere, restless at 2:00 a.m., or waking up over a cup of coffee. He's there, and his attention is in the details. Your tears are gathered by him even though you thought your pillow soaked them up. He is more than merely next to you; he is actively with you. Ears engaged, eyes open, heart ready to carry yours. He is Immanuel. God with us. In every way.

God isn't a place or time but a relational being. We can learn about and seek God in church, but where we find him is in the heart. He is not Sunday or 6:00 a.m. devotions. But he'll meet us Sunday and every day and every time we sit with him over our favorite warm drink. He'll be there. The question is, will we? Jeremiah wrote of God's promise that we'll find him when we seek him with all our hearts. God wants to be found not in a place but inside of us. Our souls awaken to the wonder of walking with God when we fully enjoy the reality of his presence. One of my favorite moments in Scripture is when Isaac went out to the field to meditate, to be present with the presence of God (Genesis 24:63). He reminds us that being with God starts with us.

So go for a walk along the beach or hop in your car and simply be with Jesus. Meditate on him. The Hebrew language has several words for meditate. One of them means "to moan or mutter," to not leave what's on your mind there but bring it out through physical expression. Let your heart interact with his. And may the pressure to do things for God not make you miss the importance of simply being with God. Love him with everything you are because he first loved you. And that kind of love wants to be together. The kind that doesn't care about where you are but who you're with. May we remember to be present with the One whose very presence lives within us.

A TASTE OF
DREAMS

*Whether you eat or drink, or whatever
you do, do all to the glory of God.*

1 CORINTHIANS 10:31

Dreams are placed on our hearts not to frustrate us but to fulfill us: "A desire fulfilled is sweet to the soul" (Proverbs 13:19). When the desire to become a personal trainer awakened in me, a little fear became loud and questioned my career choice. Is this really what God wants me to do? Do I spend my time helping people take care of a temporary body? Is what I'm doing not spiritual enough?

In the Old Testament, we see God himself filling up a worker with the Spirit of God to be an artist: "I have filled him with the Spirit of God, with ability and intelligence, with knowledge and all craftsmanship, to devise artistic designs, to work in gold, silver, and bronze, in cutting stones for setting, and in carving wood, to work in every craft" (Exodus 31:3-5).

God supernaturally fills an ordinary person to do extraordinary things. Is carving wood extraordinary? Well, look at Jesus. Before Jesus was called the "good teacher," he was a good carpenter.

Bring to fruition the gifts God has filled you with because the promise fulfilled will be **SWEET** to your soul.

Before he called his first disciples, he first learned to carve wood. Jesus wasn't beneath blue-collar work; he was a blue-collar worker himself. Don't believe the lie that the gifts God has given you aren't spiritual enough.

Again, Jesus was a carpenter, and I would guess he didn't inscribe verses on the benches he made. That would be a beautiful thing to do, but the point is, a good bench is a good bench simply because it is. Jesus was doing what the Father called him to do during that time in his life, and that was enough. Look at what famous writer and theologian C.S. Lewis had to say about this:

> The first business of a story is to be a good story. When Our Lord made a wheel in the carpenter shop, depend upon it: It was first and foremost a good wheel. Don't try to 'bring in' specifically Christian bits: if God wants you to serve him in that way (He may not: there are different vocations) you will find it coming in of its own accord. If not, well—a good story which will give innocent pleasure is a good thing, just like cooking a good nourishing meal…. *Any* honest workmanship (whether making stories, shoes, or rabbit hutches) can be done to the glory of God.*

Lewis summed up well what Paul wrote in his letter to Corinth: "So, whether you eat or drink, or whatever you do, do all to the glory of God" (1 Corinthians 10:31).

Maybe you struggle because your work doesn't seem fulfilling,

---

* Walter Hooper, ed., *The Collected Letters of C.S. Lewis*, vol. 3 (San Francisco, CA: HarperOne, 2007), 502-3.

or you believe what you're doing doesn't have purpose. Look at Paul's words carefully: Eating food can be done to the glory of God. He mentions the one thing every person on this planet must do to stay alive. And even that can be done for God. So don't listen to anyone who tells you differently, not even yourself.

Bring to fruition the gifts God has filled you with because the promise fulfilled will be sweet to your soul. God put his Spirit in man to do every form of craftsmanship—so don't write off those talents as unimportant or unspiritual. Every gift is to be opened and used. We bless others, God, and ourselves when we do what God calls us to do. It brings sweetness. It seems God wouldn't describe something as sweet without also giving us the invitation to taste it.

We know the only way food can be eaten is if it's first grown, and the only way a desire can be fulfilled is if it grows from a daydream to a plan. Take seriously the dreams God's given you. Even the mundane can mobilize the eternal, but you have to get moving. And be patient: Good things take time. Lydia, a prominent woman who sold luxury purple clothing, became a Christian and used her wealth to help fund the early church. She did not build her business in a day, but when it came time for her to serve God with it, she was ready. You're tasting the fruit of a desire right now— this devotion, this book. And I can only hope it's sweet for you. If the taste of the Lord himself is sweet and so is a fulfilled desire, then maybe God is hidden in plain sight right in the middle of our dreams. He's behind every brushstroke if only we have eyes to see. May we not believe desires are to be left unfulfilled when God is the one who fills us with them.

A TASTE OF
RENEWAL

Therefore, if anyone is in Christ, he is a new creation.
The old has passed away; behold, the new has come.

2 CORINTHIANS 5:17

The day I read about the practice of *kintsugi*, it captivated my heart. "Kin" means gold, and "tsugi" means repair, so its name implies its mission: "golden repair." This Japanese art technique repairs broken pottery by fixing the fractured parts of breakage with a precious metal, typically gold. As a philosophy, it treats brokenness and the restoration process as something not to be disguised but highlighted as part of the history of the object. It turns scars into beauty marks. I believe our hearts soften when hearing this, because who doesn't want their broken pieces glued back together? We long for our wounds to be made into something meaningful. This is redemption. We're drawn like magnets to redemption because our souls not only want it; they need it.

One of my favorite places in the world that captures the quintessential idea of restoration is a little town called Mendocino, the only town on California's coast that's designated as a historical landmark. With an enchanting coastline that hugs a magical old-growth redwood forest, this charming, simple town is completely captivating. Everything from the architecture to the overgrown flowers is reminiscent of a different time. The cottages and Victorian houses are right at home. I think how strange it would be to build a modern home in this place. The new construction would stand out—and not in a good way. It's a town made for a different time, a different world. And perhaps so are we.

Our souls long for *kintsugi* today, but they'll only be fully mended in their intended home tomorrow. The beauty of eternity is found in the promise that what we long for will someday be a reality. "But we have this treasure in jars of clay, to show that the surpassing power belongs to God and not to us" (2 Corinthians 4:7). The riches of eternity are alive in our earthen hearts, now. We hold within us the duality of being bought back and being made new. We don't quite fit in here, like an up-to-date building in an old-fashioned town. We've been redeemed to the point of being made brand new. As King Solomon wrote, "He has made everything beautiful in its time. Also, he has put eternity into man's heart" (Ecclesiastes 3:11). He makes us beautiful today, and eternity is on the horizon.

As C.S. Lewis put it, "If we find ourselves with a desire that nothing in this world can satisfy, the most probable explanation is that we were made for another world."* Eternity was set in our hearts back in the Garden of Eden. The goal from the beginning was simple: to live in relational harmony with our creator God,

---

* C.S. Lewis, *Mere Christianity* (San Francisco, CA: HarperOne, 2015), 136–37.

from every today into every tomorrow. But weeds and thorns sprang up, and we were destined to return to dust, to be forever clothed in mortality. We fought to push back the weeds and be clothed in beauty once again, but our strength withered like the flower, so we hid in shame, but nothing could have prepared us for the love we were about to meet.

The plan was clear but not painless. Our creator God decided to robe himself in his created humanity. Flesh and blood of the divine, subjected to a cross grown from the ground, in order to buy back his precious dust. His eyes saw our beauty even though we were ash, and although darkness appeared to have won, the transformation had just begun. For out of the grave, a garden began to grow. Our redeemer wore a crown of thorns so that one day thorns might never flourish again. After three days, he put death six feet under so it might never have its grip on us again. So here we are now back in the garden, although it looks different because we know the story of the soil found underneath our feet. We've been redeemed yet made new, and we know what this means: We will never again see the dirt as an end but only a reminder of the coming beginning. Because there's a gardener we know who just so happens to have a way with dust. The old has passed away. Behold, the new has come.

A TASTE OF
FORGIVENESS

Bear one another's burdens, and so fulfill the law of Christ.

GALATIANS 6:2

We become most like Jesus when we live for ourselves the least. This does not mean we don't have boundaries. Remember, even Jesus set limits in his life. It means the priority of our lives is not to gratify our flesh. When we crucify our selfish desires in pursuit of serving others, it's then we find we truly live. Right before Paul tells us to bear one another's burdens, he says, "Brothers and sisters, if someone is caught in a sin, you who live by the Spirit should restore that person gently. But watch yourselves, or you also may be tempted" (Galatians 6:1 NIV). Maybe that's exactly how we lift each other's burdens; we learn to restore others in gentleness, because within ourselves, we also can struggle with doing the things we don't want to do. It makes me think of the ultimate burden-lifter himself, who blazed the trail in what the picture of forgiveness looks like for us.

Peter loved Jesus so much, he not only didn't want him to die but also told Jesus he would die with him. His heart was to be with

Jesus in every sense of the word. But when Jesus faced the looming shadow of the cross, and push came to shove, Peter could not bear the weight of the night of the arrest. He loved his Lord and didn't want to deny him, but it seems Peter betrayed his own heart, too, when the words "I do not know him" left his lips (Luke 22:57). And so, the rooster crowed, and the sound of shame reverberated in his soul. More than anything, Peter wanted to help carry Jesus's burden because he loved him, but he tripped up and fell into temptation. He couldn't lift his own burden in that moment, let alone help lift the burden of his beloved friend, leader, and Lord.

Jesus turned to look at Peter, and when their eyes met, it filled the fisherman-turned-follower's heart with so much remorse that it spilled out as bitter tears. What was he to do now? The only plausible idea was to go back to what he knew, so he headed to the water with a fishing net in hand and regret in his heart.

A few days after Jesus's resurrection, Peter and some of the other disciples went out fishing all night but caught nothing. As morning rounded the corner, little did Peter know, new mercies did too. Jesus stood on the shore and told them to cast their net on the other side of the boat as they were coming in. Look what happened when John recognized their resurrected Lord: "That disciple whom Jesus loved therefore said to Peter, 'It is the Lord!' When Simon Peter heard that it was the Lord, he put on his outer garment, for he was stripped for work, and threw himself into the sea" (John 21:7). The second it hit Peter's ears that it was Jesus calling out to them, he didn't hesitate to throw himself into the water, clothing and all, because nothing was going to stop him from being with his Lord—not even his mistakes. As much as this story shows us the heart of Peter, perhaps even more it reveals the heart of his Lord. Jesus not only was approachable after he was betrayed but purposely sought out his disciples, with his heart set on restoring Peter.

Peter had warmed himself by a fire as a chill went through his soul on the night of the betrayal. Now he found himself around another fire as Jesus cooked him breakfast on the beach, but this time, he felt the warmth from the love that radiated from his Lord's heart. Jesus asked Peter three times if he loved him, and it seems as if Peter would know exactly what Jesus was trying to say: "Your failures don't get the last word. I do." I've always been told that as Jesus carried the cross, he thought of me. But here I think of how he remembered Peter. Perhaps that's the heart that beats behind bearing one another's burdens—that of our redeemer who lifted those burdens for us.

A TASTE OF
VICTORY

*We do not wrestle against flesh and blood, but
against the rulers, against the authorities, against
the cosmic powers over this present darkness, against
the spiritual forces of evil in the heavenly places.*

EPHESIANS 6:12

The struggle is real, but it isn't against flesh and blood. The promise inside this verse gives us an advantage in every battle we encounter in life: identifying our real opponent. The main conflict is not with one another but with our enemy whose actual mission is to steal, kill, and destroy. This has been the single most helpful lens I've ever looked through when it comes to facing opposition. Notice I say lens, not tool. We can't stand against our enemy simply by knowing who they are, but we need to know who our enemy is in order to stand: "Be sober-minded; be watchful. Your adversary the devil prowls around like a roaring lion, seeking someone to devour" (1 Peter 5:8). Our adversary is the master of deception. It says he's *like* a roaring lion, not that he is a roaring lion, and that's exactly why we're told to be watchful, which is pretty impossible to do if we're not sober minded.

Now you might wonder, *Is the devil going to pounce on me like an animal?* Metaphorically speaking, yes. Because that's what this is: a word picture of how our enemy works, so if you're aware and alert, you'll be able to "resist the devil, and he will flee from you" (James 4:7). There seems to be a lot going on here between cosmic powers and spiritual forces, but for simplicity's sake, we can confidently say we are in a spiritual battle. And the evil one—or as Jesus called him, Satan, the tempter and ruler of this world—is ultimately referenced as the father of lies, which means he is the primary driving force of darkness behind it all. Paul doesn't leave us to wonder how to overcome him: "Take up the whole armor of God, that you may be able to withstand in the evil day" (Ephesians 6:13). So we don't need to be afraid; we just need to be prepared.

This all started in Eden, and although our enemy is defeated because Jesus's death destroyed "the one who has the power of death, that is, the devil" (Hebrews 2:14), he will still try to deceive and accuse us today before he's ultimately cast out. But here's the thing: Over and over, the Scripture writers use the word "stand" when it comes to facing and being victorious over our enemy. Stand for what and how? Stand for what God represents by becoming like his Son Jesus. By abiding in him and bearing the fruit of the Spirit. We are able to oppose the works of the flesh because the Spirit produces in us love, joy, peace, patience, and all the way down to self-control (Galatians 5:22-23).

So let's get practical, starting with wisdom from James: "What causes fights and quarrels among you? Don't they come from your desires that battle within you?" (James 4:1 NIV). While the battles we'll face in life will take on all shapes and sizes, I want to give you a common example of how we can overcome these desires within ourselves that culminate in a fight or quarrel like James talks about. When I'm in an argument with someone, I remember who my real enemy is, ask the Spirit to help me become more like Jesus in the heat of the moment, and stand in the promise that Jesus will never call me to do something he will not also enable me to do. His Spirit will help me crucify my fleshly desires and be alive to Christ, so I can respond with love, patience, words seasoned with kindness and self-control, while not letting my anger rule me. Every opportunity to walk in the flesh is an opportunity to walk in the Spirit and have victory in the Spirit.

We do not need to be afraid of an already defeated enemy. Our names have been written in the Book of Life. All we have to do is confess our sin when we do give in to temptation, and God will be faithful to cleanse us from all unrighteousness (1 John 1:9). Death has lost its grip on our souls by being nailed to the tree, so even when we do fail, we are not failures. We are forgiven.

A TASTE OF
ETERNITY

For to me to live is Christ, and to die is gain.

PHILIPPIANS 1:21

What does it mean to live? Interestingly, the answer to this question is usually found at the end of our lives. Most of us will have more clarity at the end looking back than we have at the beginning, because hindsight is twenty-twenty, right? We can fill in the blank, "For me to live is ____," with endless answers, but the only way to truly live is if we choose to live for Christ. Everything else we attempt to fill up with will ultimately prove empty.

Years ago, I sat on the beach with my Bible opened in my lap and the morning sunrise in my eyes. I was there to hang out with God in his Word and to watch my husband surf. I let the Scriptures fill my soul as my toes dug into the sand. Weeks before this, I hid a certain verse from Isaiah in my heart. While I treasure being in the Word daily, memorization has always been a challenge for me, so on this particular morning, I didn't expect my knowledge of the verse to be put to the test. I also didn't expect it would fill me in a way that would empty me of meaningless pursuits and reignite what my heart beats for. The beach was mostly empty since the sun seemed to rise before most people, but a single soul approached as they strolled along the shoreline. I didn't realize he had taken notice of me because my head was in the Psalms, but his voice broke through the stillness with a peculiar invitation: "The grass withers and the flowers fade" (Isaiah 40:8 NLT). His words stirred up the same truth that had only recently been tucked away in my heart. I finished his sentence without missing a beat: "But the word of our God stands forever" (Isaiah 40:8 NLT). He never stopped walking but responded with a smile as he carried along on his way.

What just happened? I thought to myself. *How did he have the boldness to quote half a verse to me and expect me to finish it?* And that verse of all verses. What are the odds of that? I sat on the shore alone but felt God was very much with me. It's almost as if God wanted to solidify to me: The only solid thing in this life worth living for is him. The flower will fade, and the grass will wither, but the truth of God and his Word will eternally be evergreen, a solid rock to build my life upon. My soul grasped this truth as I sat there on shifting sand; the one thing that will never change in this life is him, so how could I live for anything else?

There are many beautiful things to live for, but there's only one kind of beauty that's incorruptible: A heart that loves God will never fade. If we fill our lives with flowers, their petals will one day fall. If we enjoy our days on the grass, it will eventually wither away. We walk into a florist's shop and see blooms of every kind. Their loveliness is undeniable, but so is their eventual fade. Perhaps we buy them because we know their time is short. We rush to get them into water to enjoy a little longer. We're never disappointed when they wave good-bye because we understand their purpose. Their beauty is quick, enjoyed today and gone tomorrow. We can fill our lives with flowers, or we can realize, in their death, they point us to one who fills our lives with breath. What more could we hope for? The promise of what Jesus declared is held out to us: "Everyone who lives and believes in me shall never die" (John 11:26). So we don't have to fear, because our roots reach deep into heavenly soil. Though the grass withers and the flowers fade, if we live for Christ, to die is gain. Don't mistake this place for home but take heart—we'll be there soon.

A TASTE OF
GRACIOUSNESS

*Now you must put them all away: anger, wrath,
malice, slander, and obscene talk from your mouth.*

COLOSSIANS 3:8

O ne of the most destructive things we can do to ourselves is
tear down someone else. It can feel good in the moment to
unleash anger or gossip about someone else. Then life goes
on, and we forget because we don't feel the heat when it comes
from us, but only when the fire comes at us. When we are on the
receiving end, we more fully experience the power of words to burn
things down. Look how James paints the picture of what our tongue
is capable of: "So also the tongue is a small member, yet it boasts
of great things. How great a forest is set ablaze by such a small
fire!" (James 3:5). Even a big forest is no match for a tiny spark.

I used to think I wasn't guilty of gossiping if I kept my mouth
closed. As the proverb says, "Even a fool who keeps silent is considered wise; when he closes his lips, he is deemed intelligent" (Proverbs 17:28), but I learned that others can't gossip if we don't give
their words a place to land. In other words, words can't enter ears
that are closed; the plane can't land if it doesn't have a runway. I

don't say this because I think you need to hear it; I say it because we all need to. We're all in this together, because if you don't say it, I won't hear it, and if I won't hear it, you can't say it. Because we're all part of the body of Christ, no one escapes the flames if we use our mouths to burn someone else down. Look how Paul puts it: "If the foot should say, 'Because I am not a hand, I do not belong to the body,' that would not make it any less a part of the body" (1 Corinthians 12:15). This is how we put wheels on "love your neighbor as yourself." Because the question then moves from *Should I say this?* to *Would I want this said about me?*

"Greater love has no one than this, that someone lay down his life for his friends" (John 15:13). Sacrifice is often required to be loving and gracious. An uncomfortable conversation where gossip is introduced will likely not require us to lay down our actual bodies and risk death. However, there are some other aspects of us that might have to die, such as our pride or even insecurity. Pride can easily keep us from speaking up for another, and our sense of self-preservation might keep us from showing up for a friend. Responding with grace to extend love takes boldness and obedience.

For me, one of the most life-changing ways love has moved from word to deed is by inserting my name in First Corinthians 13:4-6. I'm rewriting the verse with my name in it, but as you read it, have yours in mind: "Cambria is patient and kind; she does not envy or boast; Cambria is not arrogant or rude. She does not insist on her own way; Cambria is not irritable or resentful; she does not rejoice at wrongdoing, but rejoices with the truth." This is not meant to condemn us but to empower us to love. Remember, "there is therefore now no condemnation for those who are in Christ Jesus" (Romans 8:1). Any ounce of guilt we feel is washed off in God's grace. And by his grace, we become more like him, more like love. Remember, condemnation drives us away from the cross, but conviction draws us to it.

May we remember our own name before we say someone else's. May our speech be sweet as honey and seasoned with grace. May we use our lips to lift up rather than tear down. And may we remember the name-above-all-names who loved us to death so our names could be counted worthy to be written in the Book of Life.

Even though a big forest is no match for a tiny spark, may we remember the matchless depths of God's vast ocean of forgiveness. Let him set a fire in our souls to love him so much that others can't help but feel the warmth of his love on their skin.

A TASTE OF
THANKFULNESS

*Give thanks in all circumstances; for this is
the will of God in Christ Jesus for you.*

1 THESSALONIANS 5:18

The promise of thankfulness is found within itself: We will be full when we give thanks. Thankfulness is a choice we make in all circumstances, which ultimately brings contentment into every circumstance. It seems those who expect everything will find disappointment, but those who appreciate everything will find contentment because contentment is found only within the heart. As Paul writes to the church in Philippi, "I have learned in whatever situation I am to be content. I know how to be brought low, and I know how to abound. In any and every circumstance, I have learned the secret of facing plenty and hunger, abundance and need. I can do all things through him who strengthens me" (Philippians 4:11-13).

When I discovered the "I can do all things" verse is used in the context of contentment, it rocked my world. If we were to refocus what Paul said here, it could read like this: When I am content, in any and every circumstance, I can do all things through him who strengthens me. Paul is teaching us how contentment is like a muscle you strengthen by thanking God all the time in everything (Philippians 4:6-7).

I've found that to be true in my own life. The more thankful I am, the deeper the roots of contentment grow within my soul. This requires practice and consistency, because just like a muscle, you have to use it, or you'll lose it.

I'll never forget reading a poem years ago by Mary Stuber called "Thank God for Dirty Dishes," which helps us reframe what a sink full of dirty dishes means: We have food! We have the blessing of provision, and the proof is in that overflowing sink. That simple change of perspective is eye-opening. If we look around, there's evidence of God's goodness everywhere.

During one of my walks, the lesson of this poem poured out as a prayer. It was a crazy, busy season of life, and I was feeling overwhelmed, which is why I needed that walk. As I thought about what this busy season indicated—that I was blessed with work for my hands—a peace settled in my soul during the unsettling time. How? By simply thanking God for everything, even the things I wouldn't usually thank him for, I felt the lightness of contentment.

When we choose to be thankful, it changes the way we see our circumstances. It changes the lens through which we look at and understand the world. As I continued walking that day, I thanked God for him and for always being with me. How regularly I can take his presence for granted! Then I thanked him for everything my eyes could see, from my little dog to the warm sand beneath my feet to the ocean breeze that cooled my skin. I was on a roll.

My heart kept the list going: I was thankful for laundry because I have clothes to wear and thankful for taxes—yes, even taxes—which meant I had another year of provision. Thankful. Full. It satisfies our souls. It strengthens our gratitude. We gain everything when we're thankful for everything because "godliness with contentment is great gain" (1 Timothy 6:6).

A lie that leaves us empty is "I can be thankful only when ____." Move the period to follow the word "thankful." And then throw in an "always." Whispering a quick prayer of gratitude is better than leaving it unsaid. The world will keep telling us we need more to become satisfied. We can keep saying enough is enough. We know that "enough" always seems to mean "just a little more." If we choose to be thankful, contentment will fill us, and we'll find abundant life—not in what we hold but in who holds us. And there are a million and one reasons to tell him "Thank you."

If we choose
to be THANKFUL,
CONTENTMENT will
fill us, and we'll find
ABUNDANT life—
not in WHAT we hold
but in WHO holds us.

A TASTE OF
REFRESHMENT

As for you, brothers, do not grow weary in doing good.

2 THESSALONIANS 3:13

It's easy to hurry by this verse and pick it up like a cup of water in the middle of a race only to throw it back in a rush and carry on in our own strength. Surprise, surprise, it seems we often bring on our own weariness because we don't slow down to savor God's Word. Do we believe it's possible to avoid growing weary? Perhaps the answer lies in continuing to ask questions. Why? Because when we ask questions, we reach for the answer and simultaneously hold hands with the idea that we don't have it figured out. "I don't know" is the phrase we must constantly use as a diving board to jump into the sea of Scripture. In that declaration, we stop ourselves from leaning on our own understanding and instead acknowledge the only reliable source for answers is God. If we want to believe it's possible to avoid growing weary, we must first consider two important questions: What is good? And how do we not grow weary in doing it? We won't weary ourselves in search of the answer because our search ends before it starts if we go to the One who holds the answers and discover he is the answer.

So what is good? This question is reminiscent of another in the Bible, "What is truth?" (John 18:38). Pontius Pilate asked this of Jesus, not realizing the answer stood right in front of him. Jesus had at another time said, "I am the way, and the truth, and the life" (John 14:6). So what does the Truth say is good? "And he said to him, 'Why do you ask me about what is good? There is only one who is good'" (Matthew 19:17). There's only one who is good! As we go down the windy path of all these questions, we find the road narrows and turns the question on itself; the question isn't *what* is good but *who* is good. Who is good but God alone?

Picture Martha and Mary: One did what she thought was good, and the other sat with the one who is good. Our definition of good looks different from God's. Martha initially scolded Mary for not serving or playing hostess, and Judas scolded Mary for pouring out her perfume on Jesus's feet rather than selling that expensive perfume to give to the poor. Jesus silenced both of them. The good works we do are nothing compared to simply being with our good Lord. This is at the heart of Jesus's heart: We will not grow weary in doing good when we stop wearing ourselves out trying to do good. We are to come to him first, and after that, the good works we pursue will not weary us but will refresh others, ourselves, and God.

Jesus reiterated this when he was questioned: "Then they said to him, 'What must we do, to be doing the works of God?' Jesus answered them, 'This is the work of God, that you believe in him whom he has sent'" (John 6:28-29). Believe. That's it. We might not be able to physically sit at his feet, but we can believe in him with our hearts. If belief is what makes our heart his home, then we'll naturally open it up to others in service of him. If you're thinking, *Didn't the Bible say to be a doer and not a hearer only?* you're exactly right. We'll know what to do only if we first go to the One who is good and hear him say, "If you love me, you will keep my commandments" (John 14:15). And what's the greatest commandment? To love him with all our heart and to love our neighbor as ourselves. That kind of love moves from words to actions because that's how we ourselves would want to be loved.

After our deep dive, it's time to come up for air. May we breathe in the refreshment that comes when we take the time to slow down and savor God's Word. I hope you've found that while the answer is simple, it's also deeply complex. Don't be afraid to "work out your own salvation" (Philippians 2:12), because it's when we do that kind of work, weariness is replaced with abiding rest.

A TASTE OF
HEALTH

While bodily training is of some value, godliness
is of value in every way, as it holds promise for
the present life and also for the life to come.

1 TIMOTHY 4:8

I used to live my life starting on Monday. My initial takeoff into health and fitness was bumpy. My goal was simple: to take care of my body. But things quickly took a turn as dissatisfaction settled in my heart every time I looked in the mirror. Comparison crept in, and the gap between where I was and where I wanted to be felt far and wide. That distance made me feel deep discontentment. To quiet the war within me, I pushed myself in the gym to my physical limit. Every day. Overexercise became normal, and I restricted the food on my plate because I thought it would bring freedom to my soul.

This verse establishes that bodily training is of some value; however, it became the only thing I valued. I prayed to God as I popped a diet pill and said, "I can do all things through Christ who strengthens me," and then pushed myself beyond my physical limits by doing a high-intensity workout on the treadmill. The problem was that no matter how hard I tried, it was never enough because I was chasing something that wasn't there. A perfect body promised me happiness, and I believed her. On my way to pursue "healthy and happy," I got very lost. I got lost trying to follow a perfect diet and trying to make sure I never missed a day of exercise. I got so lost, I found myself binge eating on my bedroom floor with a stomach so full I was sick but a spirit so empty I finally cried out to God. On the floor of my room with tearstained cheeks and a worn-out soul, I surrendered my image to the One who created me in his.

The crash landing hurt, but I felt grateful to be back on the ground. This body was created by God and given to me to be treated as a gift—not worshipped as a god. I was ready to stop worshipping myself. Renewing my mind with truth became a fight I didn't realize would require such perseverance. One night, I broke down to one of my youth leaders and told her how much I still struggled. She looked straight into my eyes and spoke what felt like a lifeline to my soul: "The LORD will fight for you; you need only to be still" (Exodus 14:14 NIV). Those words changed everything. I knew I wanted Jesus not only as my Savior but as the Lord of my life. With him, I had everything I wanted. He satisfied my soul. He became my bread and water. He rescued me from the prison I had made. He fought for me and became, once again, my first love. He even turned my own destructive behavior for good and redeemed a part of my life I once thought was broken beyond repair.

And he can do that for you too.

Bodily training became of some value when it stopped being the number one thing I placed my value in. When it's in the right spot, it can be a life-giving rhythm. Let's take a step back and ask ourselves, "How can we make caring for both spirit and body not just a priority on to-do lists but a priority in our hearts?"

The little things like a quick workout, a walk around your neighborhood, and a nourishing meal aren't so little when you rush through life neglecting them. Success is not about doing it all but about asking God to enable you to care for yourself because today is all we got. Walk with God. Move your body. Will it be perfect? No, but perfect is nothing more than a lie that stands between us and showing up for our life. The perfect time will never come, and that alone can be the greatest motivator to move toward being intentional with the minutes he's given you. Because these minutes make up our life. Let's not wait to live that life on Monday but live it today and every day we wake up and find God has put breath in our lungs.

A TASTE OF
PERSEVERANCE

*I have fought the good fight, I have finished
the race, I have kept the faith.*

2 TIMOTHY 4:7

I found myself at a stoplight as a car pulled up in the lane next to me. I didn't pay attention to the car until the driver started inching closer and closer to the vehicle in front of her, and as she did, she'd slam on the brakes. I was nervous just watching. *Slow down*, I thought. We're all trying to get where we need to go, but this isn't the way to do it. Red lights demand patience, and you don't have another option except to wait, unless you want an expensive ride to an auto repair shop. Clearly, this woman wasn't able to contain the hurry inside of her because it spilled out all over the road. She was on a mission to nowhere fast. You'll never imagine what happened next. This woman got so impatient, she pulled down her car mirror, started fixing her hair, and then missed the light when it finally turned green! Her impatience made her miss the very thing she was waiting for. I couldn't help but laugh at how dramatic this whole thing was, and I had to laugh even harder when I realized I do this too. (Not literally, you get the road we're heading down. Pun intended.)

Even though this is a lighthearted story and outcome, it shows how God is always teaching us something if only we'll notice. When Jesus said, "Look at the birds of the air" (Matthew 6:26), he was preparing to teach the common people around him using an example they could relate to immediately. This is the beauty of a parable. We learn from what we know and can see. Real-time parables happen all around, even today. So we're told to fight the good fight, to run the race, to keep our faith, and we can't do that if we let impatience drive a wedge between us and our goal. We can't give up so quickly; we can't give up at all. We run as the Scriptures encourage us to: "Lay aside every weight, and sin which clings so closely, and let us run with endurance the race that is set before us" (Hebrews 12:1). We can't let whatever it is—whether sin, or impatience, or fear of not running fast enough, or comparison to what others are doing, or worrying we won't be good enough—keep us from running. Throw off the weights. And run hard. Because we only get one race to shine as bright as we can to point others to the light of the world.

Even Jesus told us a parable of a man who gave talents—money—to his servants and specifically scolded the one servant who didn't go out and make use of his. What good is a gift if it's not put to use? Problem was, this servant was afraid to invest it or trade it out of worry he might lose it. His plan? To bury the talent in the ground so he wouldn't get ripped off and it wouldn't get lost or stolen. When the man came back to see how each of them did, he couldn't believe that this one servant had hidden underground the only talent given to him. He could have at least invested it in the bank to get interest money! We hear him say at the end, "For to everyone who has will more be given, and he will have an abundance. But from the one who has not, even what he has will be taken away" (Matthew 25:29). Fear paralyzed him, but let's feel the fear and run anyway because Jesus reminds us in this parable it's your best effort that counts, not perfection.

Don't let impatience or fear of falling make you quit. Finish the race. Give us what you've got for the sake of the world. Let God light a fire in your soul for the sake of the kingdom.

A TASTE OF
RIGHTEOUSNESS

*He saved us, not because of works done by us in
righteousness, but according to his own mercy, by the
washing of regeneration and renewal of the Holy Spirit.*

TITUS 3:5

Some words in the Scriptures are tossed around like a big Scripture word salad: righteousness, grace, mercy, justification, sin, and works. The overarching story of God's redemptive work can be missed if we get lost in this sea of words. That is to say, the gravity of what God has done for the world is told to us in a story, but it's much more than just words on a page: It's living and active. It's alive with God-breathed words that enable us to inhale life as it exhales the invitation to follow the One who has the power to breathe eternal life into us. A resurrecting breath so strong it makes us come alive in a way that death no longer has power over us.

The Bible is not a religious manual on how to get to heaven through human performance. It's a story of God's redemption of his creation—a creation he loves so much, he sacrificed himself for it. Why? Because he loves us, his image-bearers. And one day, not only we but all creation will be made new. It will be set free with no more overtaking thorns or weeds. Yes, even nature itself will be redeemed as the perfect garden it was intended to be.

This big, beautiful story of God is still unfolding today and is something we get invited into by God's grace. A relationship with God requires righteousness. But there's a huge problem: "There is no one righteous, not even one" (Romans 3:10 NIV). There's dirt on our hands and all over the floor of our hearts. That's our righteousness before God because when we tried to be righteous, we "missed the mark," or sinned. We can try to stand up straight, but our very souls are bent out of shape. God in his love doesn't leave us to pay for our sins; he knows we can't. There is nothing we can do to pay for our sins. Just as 1 + 2 will never equal 5, our works will never be able to add up to righteousness. This is exactly what Paul says here in his letter to Titus, that we're saved by God's mercy, as seen on the cross, not by works done by us in righteousness.

Interestingly, this letter is heavily focused on good works, being a doer of God's Word and not a hearer only. So if you pick out a single verse and don't put it into the context of the universal story, the beauty of it gets lost. Imagine it like a movie. It's made to be watched from beginning to end. That's not a requirement of course, but it would be pretty frustrating if movie theaters only let you inside for the last thirty minutes, right? God's Word is the same way.

In the opening scene of this letter, Paul writes, "They profess to know God, but they deny him by their works" (Titus 1:16). Our works don't save us; they simply point to the One who did. This is at the heart of why our slow-to-anger Jesus finally flipped tables: The religious elites who professed to know God continually took advantage of people who sought God. Guess who Jesus was friends with? Sinners. The ones who didn't profess to know God but confessed their need for him. Today that means the ones not looking to be saved by their works but to have the life of their Savior be at work in them.

You and I will not ever be saved by our works, but we will be known by them. May we point people to Jesus not by telling them what to do but by using our hands to point them to his heart. Our works can't buy righteousness any more than money can. If we try to make others work harder to get more, we'll exchange our cheap goodness for God's rich, free grace. And may our actions continually point to the One who freely paid our debt so we could drink of the living water: "Come, everyone who thirsts, come to the waters; and he who has no money, come, buy and eat! Come, buy wine and milk without money and without price" (Isaiah 55:1). Everyone is welcome at his table. Come and grab a seat.

A TASTE OF
CHANGE

*Accordingly, though I am bold enough in Christ
to command you to do what is required, yet
for love's sake I prefer to appeal to you.*

PHILEMON 1:8-9

There's a lot of inescapable stuff we might want to avoid, but it's necessary. There's laundry, work, cooking, paying bills, cleaning . . . I'll stop there to spare you the never-ending list. On the other hand, there are things we should do but don't always want to do or remember to do, like pray for ourselves and others, read and study the Scriptures, eat and move to stay healthy, and that list goes on too. Why is it so hard to do the things we know we should? How do we change that? It seems like right when we move toward change, it happens again: We give up. We lose motivation and go back to our usual ways, even though everything inside of us screams for it to be different.

Deep down, we want to do and be all we were created for. So we're told to try harder. Sometimes we're told to do the new thing for twenty-one days until it becomes a habit. But if we only needed to focus on behavior change, we'd all be motivation machines. The truth is, we're not machines. If we lean into the Creator's design, we'll find a clue for the solution hidden in plain sight. We're human beings. Not human doings. To change anything happening on the outside, we start on the inside. We need a renovation of the heart. And most of us respond to an appeal to that heart—not a command, not a reprimand, but a request made in the purest form, an invitation wrapped in love. Paul knew this and so did Jesus.

This is why it's so radical when we let Jesus into our lives because we do so through the door of our hearts. An invitation for change waits on the other side. Even if it's been a while since we've let him in, he patiently stands outside our door. We hear his knock and reach for the handle. All the change we've wanted to make but haven't is laid out for him to see. Unfulfilled dreams, unused talents, and a dusty Bible sit on the shelf next to a jar of unspoken prayers and unheard requests we wanted to share but that never got past our lips.

To our surprise, Jesus walks in, yet condemnation never enters the room. His unconditional love and embrace find us in the middle of our mess as we remind ourselves "This is his home." He's not a guest; he's a resident, our long-acquainted friend. We pick up where we left off, and before he can sit down, our heart spills out before him because we realize how much we've missed him. We ask him question after question, and as he answers with grace, an unexpected tear makes its way down our cheek . . . we remember just how kind he really is. He never once looks around at the room; his gaze is fixed on us as he listens. He then leans over to catch our lone tear, and our heart fills with remorse as we lower our head, wondering to ourselves, *Why did I close him out for so long?*

We look up to discover nothing is the same. Our prayer jar once filled with need after need and question after question is empty. Our dreams are written out. Even the dust has left the building. This place and all that fills it is nothing more than a mirror of our own soul. We realize we're made completely new in Christ. Without him at home, our heart is nothing more than a house. The truest part of our being is made alive once again because as soon as he walked in, so did we.

So how do we do what we really want to do? We must first be who we really are. A new creation, in God himself. Because it's then we find we don't just write; we become an author. We don't just dance; we become a dancer. We don't just run; we become a runner. When we're in Christ, he changes who we are, which naturally changes what we do. As Jesus said, "The good person out of the good treasure of his heart produces good, and the evil person out of his evil treasure produces evil, for out of the abundance of the heart his mouth speaks" (Luke 6:45). What we do flows from who we are. The dream of doing and being all that's in our hearts begins when we let him into ours.

A TASTE OF
ENDURANCE

*Let us then with confidence draw near to the
throne of grace, that we may receive mercy
and find grace to help in time of need.*

HEBREWS 4:16

The famous picture of young John Jr. curiously peeking out from underneath his father's desk captured America's heart. Why? Because to us, John F. Kennedy is Mr. President, but to John Jr., he is Dad. If anybody else dared to get that close to the Oval Office without permission, they would be immediately escorted away. But because of who the boy is and whose he is, he has not only full access but full confidence to crawl underneath that iconic desk. No one would ever say that what he's doing is even remotely disrespectful or irreverent because that would be ridiculous. He's his son.

That is how we are to come to our Father in heaven.

As children of God, confidence is not something we need but something we have. I love how John Mark Comer painted this picture of confidence in coming to God our Father: "When I get home from work, my kids don't bow down and crawl up to kiss

Because of GRACE, this is a no-strings-attached kind of LOVE. It's not based on our COMMITMENT to God but on his COVENANT with us.

my feet. Sadly. They run and jump into my arms—'Daddy!'"*
We're invited to know this kind of confident love and see it, as the
apostle John writes, "See what kind of love the Father has given
to us, that we should be called children of God; and so we are"
(1 John 3:1). Even when people brought children to see Jesus, his
disciples tried to keep them from approaching him, but he pushed
back, saying, "Let the little children come to me and do not hin-
der them, for to such belongs the kingdom of heaven" (Matthew
19:14). Even with the disciples' firsthand experience with Jesus's
love, their immediate response when they saw kids running toward
their rabbi was to protect their Lord's time and energy. They didn't
realize what they were actually doing was keeping the very heirs
of the kingdom out. Let's open our eyes wide and see that this is
the nature of our relationship with God.

Maybe you don't feel like that. Maybe you feel like you've disappointed your Father. Like you've exhausted his patience, love,
and grace. Remember that before we came to him, he came to us.
Who ran after who in the prodigal son story? We both know it
wasn't the son. Not even the potent smell of pig could keep the
father from wrapping his arms around his son (Luke 15:20). The
only reason we'll ever hide from the love of God is if we forget: He.
Is. Our. Father. The only thing that can ever separate us from his
love? Maybe we'll never fully comprehend that the answer is . . .
nothing. Not death, life, angels, principalities, powers, things present, things to come, height, depth, any and every creature—shall I

---

* John Mark Comer, *God Has a Name* (Grand Rapids, MI: Zondervan, 2017), 151.

go on?—will ever be able to separate us from his love. Because of grace, this is a no-strings-attached kind of love. It's not based on our commitment to God but on his covenant with us.

We do not need to be afraid to run into the arms of our Father, because he first ran after us. He is not unaware and unmerciful of our failure to follow him; he left the whole flock to go after our wandering hearts. And that can only mean one thing. Do not believe any lie is louder than God's love for you. No matter what a child does, their DNA never changes. No matter how long it's been, may we confidently draw near to the throne of God and find with every step closer, our eyes can't escape the fact, "Hey, that's my dad."

A TASTE OF
JOY

Count it all joy, my brothers, when you
meet trials of various kinds.

JAMES 1:2

I'm not spiritually mature enough to joyfully suffer." My brother-in-law's words echoed from the living room and made their way into my soul. Me neither. Instead of concealing his vulnerability, he let the honesty in his heart spill from his lips. I'd rather not think about my worst fears being brought to life, and I can imagine that probably makes two of us. So while we know Jesus told us not to worry about the future, he also said the dark, thorny path—the valley of the shadow of death—is clearly on the map as part of the journey. Yet he assured us we'd never walk alone. So how do we hold both pain and promise? The duality seems hard to wrap our hearts around.

Math isn't my strong point, but basic addition tells me that trials plus testing wouldn't add up to joy. My brother-in-law's statement probed a question within my heart. Is it true? Do we honestly believe that every part of what God says can be trusted? Is it possible for our frail human hearts to count trials as joy as our Creator invites us to? What if joy is found not in a perfect life but in the hope of eternal life—a gift, by the way, only made possible to us through the suffering of our Savior.

What if present pain doesn't change the tune of hallelujah but turns it up? What if the woman in labor's contractions is a physical expression of hope itself? She can absolutely be confident her greatest joy is coming because her hour has come. She endures the momentary affliction for a joy far beyond comparison. Of course, the baby who caused her sorrow won't make her bitter toward them at birth; she'll forget what she just endured because joy has been born. I rejoiced with my sister when she finally went into labor, not because of her pain but because of the coming promise. Every cry from her lips and pain in her body brought her closer to a love like no other. Just when we think a joyful life is exclusively found in an existence free of suffering, we're reminded that life's greatest joy comes forth through it.

We can hold on today because of the incomparable joy tomorrow holds. Jesus showed us exactly this with his life crowned not with ease but with thorns. He walked not on a paved path but on a rugged road with a wooden cross. His life wasn't pain-free but purpose-filled, which enabled him to endure current sorrow for the coming joy. And we're invited to look "to Jesus, the founder and perfecter of our faith, who for the joy that was set before him endured the cross" (Hebrews 12:2) so we might endure too. Because even though his only robe would be gambled away, he'd soon be robed in glory forever. And even though his friends abandoned him, he'd be their friend to the end, never leaving them, so they might receive life abundantly. His name was mocked so ours could be permanently marked in the Book of Life. And then he rose so that we could rise. We can hold on because he never let go of us.

So how are both pain and promise held? We see that the promise is found inside the pain. Not separate but one, not sorrow but joy. His stripes are where we find healing. His cross is where we find mercy. His nails are where we find forgiveness. His grave is where we find life. So we can say *Hallelujah!*—an expression of joy—even in the shadow of death because the shadow is nothing more than proof of the sunlight. Life is on its way, so don't be afraid to sing in the darkness. Because hallelujah is not just any kind of noun; it's an interjection. It doesn't relate grammatically to any other part of the sentence. It stands alone. It interrupts. It appears suddenly. And it ends with an exclamation. So take heart, not because you'll never walk through the shadows, but because when you do, you can listen closely to hear the echo of joy—*Hallelujah!*—bringing light in the middle of your darkest valley.

A TASTE OF
GOODNESS

*Like newborn infants, long for the pure spiritual
milk, that by it you may grow up into salvation—
if indeed you have tasted that the Lord is good.*

1 PETER 2:2-3

I don't know about you, but I eat a lot of food. Imagine trying to survive on the occasional cupcake: As good as they are, it goes without saying that it wouldn't be enough to satisfy.

Our souls simply can't thrive only having God's Word from time to time. We find ourselves worn out, weary, and weighed down with burdens, when all along, he invites us to the table to be fortified with his goodness. Most of us don't even realize we're undernourished.

For years, I bought into the idea that my body could function on thin air. Fasting moved from an occasional practice to a way of life for me. Protein? Carbs? Fat? We didn't meet until the very end of the day. It's taken me years to realize my body knows me better than I know myself. Its signals are the brilliant design of the Creator, and they lead me to nourishment when I pay attention.

God made our bodies extremely resilient. They're so resourceful that when they lack resources, they tap into the backup generator of me, myself, and I. If we don't eat, our bodies will begin to break down. No glucose for fuel? How about some muscle for a snack? No calcium coming in? Time to break down those pearly whites. It's impossible to thrive without food; when we try, we enter survival mode. The craziest thing of all is we might not even know when we're in survival mode! No, it's not an alternate reality we're living in. It's just cortisol and adrenaline making their way through our blood so we don't stop to pull out the nail we just stepped on as we run away from the bear that's right behind us. Stress hormones feel good. They make us numb to pain. They give us endurance. That's their job. But what eventually happens? What goes up must come down.

No one needs to tell you when you're thirsty because that's your body's job. In the same way, Jesus said it's the Holy Spirit's job to "convict the world regarding sin . . . because they do not believe in Me" (John 16:8-9 NASB). It would be very strange if I were to go around and tell other people that they need water; the need is as clear as the water itself. Now that I am a nutrition coach, people ask me questions about healthy eating all the time to help guide them into deeper nourishment. (And I do encourage them to drink water!) They have lots of questions, and it's my joy to be their guide and help. I don't expect them to know about stress hormones and gluconeogenesis, because that's my job, not theirs.

Our need for Jesus—who is both our bread and water—is innate because of the Holy Spirit's work in us. But it is up to us to come to him for daily sustenance, to know him and be nourished by him and his goodness. And here's the greatest part: Jesus is both our daily bread and our guide; he sustains us every step of the way and directs our every step. It's like having a coach who guides you in exactly how to eat and then prepares all the food for you. Your job is easy. Just follow his lead and stay hungry.

May we follow Jesus every day so he can fill us. Don't do it out of obligation but because of the invitation to taste the nourishing love he freely gives. The hunger inside will remind us we have a seat at his table. He waits for us each day to dine with him. May we say yes to a nourished soul.

A TASTE OF
DISCIPLESHIP

*For this very reason, make every effort to supplement
your faith with virtue, and virtue with knowledge.*

2 PETER 1:5

We don't have to take supplements, but they can be helpful in the world we live in. Our soil and water are depleted of minerals they once had, which makes our food not as nourishing as it's supposed to be. While it's not a requirement, there is wisdom in helping our body do its job. It's the same for our spiritual health too. God fulfilled the promise to give us everything we need to be sustained in life and then goes on to invite us to supplement our faith. Is supplementation required? Nope. But it does open a door into deeper nourishment, so wouldn't we be curious to step forward in that?

Today's scripture tells us to make every effort to supplement our faith. I think of it as Peter's way of telling us to put the pill organizer out on the counter, so forgetting becomes hard to do. We're specifically told to supplement faith with virtue, then add knowledge, self-control, steadfastness, and finally, love. Each element builds on the next, giving us the ability to grow and be fruitful:

"For if these qualities are yours and are increasing, they keep you from being ineffective or unfruitful in the knowledge of our Lord Jesus Christ" (2 Peter 1:8).

My baby niece recently started eating solid food. She can stay on the milk, but my sister offers her a variety of food now so she can have a wider range of vitamins and minerals to become the healthiest she can be. Again, the same goes for us spiritually. When we are nourished by more than bread alone but every word that comes from the mouth of God, our growth will be obvious as we move from being a follower of Jesus to a disciple of Jesus.

Disciple means "disciplined one," and our development from follower to disciple requires us to be disciplined to pursue more of what we need. Spiritually, we can choose to stay babies, or we can step into maturity in Christ to experience the fullness of a fruitful life in him. We grow from knowing Jesus is the way to practicing the way of Jesus. When we let him be both our *Adonai* (or Lord) and our *rabbi* (or teacher), then we become his students. Jesus gently welcomes us, "Take my yoke upon you, and learn from me" (Matthew 11:29). Jesus invites us to come to him, then follow him, and finally learn more of him and his way and then do what we've been taught. We can choose to stay a follower or take up his yoke and grow into all he created for us to be.

Just as babies move from pure milk to solids, we mature as we continue to abide in Christ: "For everyone who lives on milk is unskilled in the word of righteousness, since he is a child. But solid food is for the mature, for those who have their powers of discernment trained by constant practice to distinguish good from evil" (Hebrews 5:13-14). Did you know that one of the only foods babies can't eat is honey? They need to be older for it to be safe to eat. What a perfect illustration. As we go from being followers to disciples, we move from milk to honey. As the psalmist said, "How sweet are your words to my taste, sweeter than honey to my mouth!" (Psalm 119:103). The Word of God is like honey reaching our cells, the purest source of energy that provides exactly what we need to produce good fruit in our lives.

It's not a baby's fault they can't eat honey until they've grown and matured physically enough to have its sweetness. It's not our fault we're not ready to bear fruit until we've grown our roots deeper into the words of Jesus. As we do, we don't need to be afraid of the honey anymore because we've matured and are ready to taste, see, and step into the fruition of a life lived in the full goodness of God as a disciple of Jesus, the Christ. Let's be not just hearers but doers. Let's step out further from following and say yes to being a disciple. It will be the sweetest yes of your life.

A TASTE OF
FAITHFULNESS

*Little children, let us not love in word or
talk but in deed and in truth.*

1 JOHN 3:18

There aren't a lot of conversations I remember having with my grandmother. She went to be with Jesus when I was eighteen, and while I wish I had the treasure of some of her words of wisdom, the reality is, I can't recall a specific conversation. But I do remember what she did. During my childhood, my mom was very sick with an autoimmune disease. Because of the illness, my sister and I stayed at my grandmother's house often. My grandma was up every day at 4:00 a.m. By the moment our sleepy eyes found their way open, she had the coffeepot going, hair rollers in, Bible open, a sermon on the TV, rose garden tended to, and breakfast ready. Her number one priority was taking care of us. She wanted nothing more than to meet our needs. And not just meet them but exceed them. Her actions were visible proof of her love. Her words were nothing more than the icing on the cake. But to frost a cake, you first have to bake one. One thing builds on the other.

When you say you love someone with your lips, but your actions don't align with your words, the math doesn't add up.

I love you + I won't do anything to show it doesn't equal love.

Jesus didn't just *say* I love you; he went to the cross. He didn't just tell us to love our enemies; he washed Judas's feet. He didn't just tell us to not love money; he flipped tables in the temple when worship became more about revenue than relationship. His talk wasn't cheap. His words had power because his actions gave them weight. His final word was the action of the cross. It is finished. When Jesus says he loves you, he means it with his life.

And maybe I should keep this a secret, but sometimes, I find what Jesus did far more curious than what he said. There's something about watching someone walk. We are invited into Jesus's inner circle as we get to see his words lived out through his life in the Gospels. What he says and does shows us who he is: love. It adds up. The incarnation of love teaches us how not to love too: with words alone. And so he loves. He touches, heals, binds up wounds, and draws near to the brokenhearted. He bends down to wash feet and stands up for the oppressed. He might have looked at my grandma and smiled as she scooped up Neapolitan ice cream, put a bandage on my knee, and wiped my tears. Because he does the same for us. We're his kids. And like a good father, he doesn't just talk the talk; he walks the walk.

I believe God uses so much physical imagery in the Bible because he wants us to truly grasp the extent of his love. He really does want to carry the burden that broke your heart. He wants to lift your head when your soul is weighed down. And he is ready to catch your anxieties in a bottle when they fall as tears. Think about that: Your tears move the heart of God in a way that makes his hand reach out to collect every drop of pain (Psalm 56:8). His love ensures no pain goes unseen or untouched by him. The heart of God is on clear display, seen in the bottle of your tears he keeps on his shelf. Yes, yours. Why? Because of love.

Receiving this kind of love from Jesus does something in our hearts; it doesn't just make us better; it makes us whole. In return, he asks that we love him with all our heart, soul, mind, and strength and then share that love with others. May our every "I love you" move past lip service and into service to honor the faithfulness of the One who showed us how. May we feel the love of God in the same way the sun warms our skin; may it be real and tangible and make us want to invite everyone else into its rays.

A TASTE OF
DELIGHT

*I rejoiced greatly to find some of your children walking in
the truth, just as we were commanded by the Father.*

2 JOHN 1:4

D o we know how deeply God delights in us? One day at the
beach, I noticed a father helping his three-year-old learn to
catch some waves. Their simple goal was for his son to stand
up on the board. I could tell they both were determined to make
it happen. After countless failed attempts, their plan remained
unchanged: Don't give up. It was their unwavering perseverance
against the sea that gave them the chance to succeed. All of a sudden, a resounding burst of applause roared as the boy rode the long-
board over the whitewash and all the way to shore. The father was a
crowd of one, and he cheered so loud and proud to make up for it.

As I watched this unfold, I had an odd thought: *Was he the
best surfer on the beach?* What an irrelevant question, right? And
yet it hit me. Maybe this is how God delights in us: "The LORD
directs the steps of the godly. He delights in every detail of their
lives. Though they stumble, they will never fall, for the LORD holds
them by the hand" (Psalm 37:23-24 NLT). Though we're afraid to

get in the water, fall off the board a thousand times, and worry we're not the best surfer on the beach, it doesn't stop our Father from taking great delight in us.

We're not going to do everything perfectly, but may we always remember that when we fall, we fall into grace. It's his joy to pick us up. His delight is constant, just like the waves that never stop rolling in. His joy is deeper than the ocean itself, and his grace is as endless as the horizon. His thoughts for us quite literally outnumber the grains of sand on all the beaches on all the earth. We can't wrap our hearts around his delight because his heart for us is bigger than we can imagine. It's easy to feel skeptical of God's love for us. We wonder how it's possible he can delight in our lives when they're clearly full of fear and failure. But as I watched this father-son moment unfold, the truth was inescapable: God delights in us because he's a good Father, not because we're perfect kids. No good father expects perfection from his child. In fact, he knows they'll mess up, make mistakes, get scared—that's why God's heart for us is clearly written out in Scripture. Kids need to be told things over and over for them to understand something, so over and over we're told, "Do not fear, I'll direct your steps, I go before you, I'm rich in mercy and grace, I love you." As the father helped the little boy get back on the board each time, he did so not in frustration but in hope and belief that his boy would absolutely be able to ride the wave. That's exactly what God does for us.

The waves will rise. We will be faced with lies that try to hold us back from "walking in the truth" (2 John 1:4) that our Father is good and is with us. We will be tempted to believe we are not worthy of God's mercy, love, grace, forgiveness, and goodness. But it seems as if God would say to us, *Look at creation itself and remember that I "assigned the sea its limit"* (Proverbs 8:29), *and then remember I've told you my goodness and mercy are limitless.* As Psalm 23:6 reminds us, his goodness and mercy will follow us. Forever.

We don't need to believe we're a disappointment when we keep falling. And we don't need to look around and compare ourselves to anyone else out there, because there is no room for comparison in the heart that is satisfied in God. May we find satisfaction not in our performance but in the fact that we delight the heart of our Father despite it. Even Jesus had words for Peter when comparison crept into his disciple's heart: "What is that to you? You follow me!" (John 21:22). All it takes for us to delight the heart of God is the simple act of us reaching for his hand. Let's get lost in his love and watch our worry, failure, and comparison get lost out at sea.

A TASTE OF
WELLNESS

*Beloved, I pray that all may go well with you and that you
may be in good health, as it goes well with your soul.*

3 JOHN 1:2

What does "wellness" really mean? I love how John goes deeper here than "good health" and ends his prayer with a kind of wellness that's found within the soul. Isn't that what we all crave, for all to be well? For wellness to reach every crack and crevice of who we are, even the furthest corner of our souls? The question is, *How does this happen?*

Jesus showed us how to nurture the soul with regular alone time with the Father, prayer, being in the house of God, honoring the Sabbath, and being deeply rooted in Scripture, and then he says, "Follow me." We're never demanded to do these things, but Jesus says, "If you love me, you will keep my commandments" (John 14:15). There is a difference between a demand and a command. Imagine someone shouting at a room of people to be quiet. They demand control but don't have authority over the room; they try to create silence from the outside in. Now picture a leader walking in, and suddenly, the room is so still you could hear a pin drop;

their presence naturally commands authority, and people aren't forced into silence—silence is created from the inside out. It's the difference between the student who sits in class because they have to and the student who reads on a topic of interest because they want to. Both are students, but one does it out of obligation, and one does it out of invitation and desire. You will never find the Scriptures demanding you read your Bible and pray every day, but you will see Jesus doing those things. Jesus even taught us to specifically ask for our daily bread so we recognize we can't find food for our souls outside of our Father in heaven. True nourishment comes from seeking first the kingdom of God.

And if we seek the kingdom first, we won't have to worry about our bodies or food because God will take care of us. Our concern is just whether we are a good steward of the gifts we've been given: "Therefore I tell you, do not be anxious about your life, what you will eat or what you will drink, nor about your body, what you will put on. Is not life more than food, and the body more than clothing?" (Matthew 6:25). For most of my life though, life was food and my body. Fitness used to be skin-deep for me. My goal in working out was to change the outside with the hope of feeling better on the inside. I struggled to separate my identity from the mirror because I had bought into what we're told and sold. From nearly every voice we hear that the harder we strive to see changes in the mirror, the happier our hearts will be. There's one major flaw in that theory because the mirror can't reflect the heart. That's not where God looks, so we shouldn't look for our solution there either.

It was only after I turned my eyes away from the mirror that I began taking care of my body in light of the truth that we aren't put here to perfect our image. It was then I found what I was really looking for: rest. Not rest because my body looked a certain way. But I received rest because my heart was freed by the truth. Free from the scale. Free from the mirror. Free to nurture my body as a gift from God. Not something to be worshipped but something to be cared for in love and with grace.

May we celebrate how we get to care for our bodies and souls rather than break under the demand that we *have to* care for them. This is when the striving ceases and the rest begins and never ends. You won't worry if you miss a workout or whether your one-sentence prayer is good enough. We can let go of the belief that joy is found on the other side of a number on a scale or that an authentic walk with God is found in how much we do for him.

We won't be remembered for what we looked like or how many verses we memorized but for the measure of how well we loved. And when we walk in true love, it will spill over into action—whatever we do will become a life-giving rhythm of wellness. So don't worry about your life or your body. Is not life . . . more?

Jesus even taught us
to specifically ASK for
our daily bread so we
recognize we can't find
food for our souls outside
of our Father in heaven.
TRUE NOURISHMENT
comes from seeking first
the kingdom of God.

A TASTE OF
HONESTY

*Now to him who is able to keep you from
stumbling and to present you blameless before
the presence of his glory with great joy . . .*

JUDE 1:24

elf-perception will forever be shaky ground to stand on,
which is why we've been invited to build our lives on a
firm foundation of truth. Imagine the details you'd focus
on to plan and build your dream home. You would picture the
layout, the paint colors, which windows face the morning sunrise, and where to place the deck to watch the sun slip beyond the
edge of the earth each night. Unless you're the builder, the condition of the foundation isn't likely a part of the dreaming stage.
Yet the promise of a good foundation is what enables us to make
a house a home. Without it, we don't have a dream ready to rise
but wood ready to fall.

I love that Jesus invites us to build our lives on him without
sugarcoating what that life will be. He doesn't say there won't be
rain or wind but acknowledges that when the storm comes—and
it will—our house will stand because of who it's built on. This

Scripture reminds us that God is able to keep us from stumbling, but that doesn't mean we never stumble. To be blameless means you're without fault: He wouldn't need to present us blameless if we were that way in and of ourselves. He is able to keep us from falling because he has never fallen. He is able to present us as blameless because he is blameless. He is honest with us and says "I'm able to keep you from stumbling" instead of "You are capable of never falling."

Honest friends make the best of friends. Don't you love those kinds of people? The kind who ask you how you are and want more than a quick answer of "Good." They'd rather have messy than fake. They'd rather see your scars and wipe your tears than watch you hide behind a facade. They're not going to fall for the idea that you've never fallen, and they'll love you anyway. This is the kind of friend Jesus is to us. He doesn't want small talk because real love is deep. You can't dive into real friendship with someone if you or they stay on the surface.

Even though he knows everything about us, there's always refreshment to be found in our time with him. The longest conversation presented in Scripture is between Jesus and the Samaritan woman at the well. That encounter was so powerful and refreshing that she left the well and told the entire town, "Come, see a man who told me all that I ever did. Can this be the Christ?" (John 4:29). Not "Come and see a man who judged me to condemnation." Not "Come and see a man who shamed me for my past." No. *Come and see a man named Jesus who knew every part of me and still loved me.* This was a life-changing conversation because "God did not send his Son into the world to condemn the world, but in order that the world might be saved through him" (John 3:17).

Who were the people Jesus couldn't have a deep conversation with? The ones who pretended to have it all together. The ones who tried to clean up the outside but were a mess on the inside. His conversations with them were real, but they couldn't go deep because the people with hearts guarded to protect their image couldn't see the truth that they were broken and needed a Savior to make them whole. Jesus called out the Scribes and Pharisees, the religious elite, for trying to clean up with their own self-righteousness and for making others try to do the same. These leaders were perfect in one way—they were perfect hypocrites because they put on a pretty convincing show. I think Jesus is saddened by hypocrisy because he wants us to reveal our brokenness so he can fill our cracked cups with living water. When he offers to fill you, let him. And don't answer his "How are you?" with "Good." Instead, let the words spill from your lips and let Jesus pour you another cup. He'll scoot a little closer to hear your heart, as you'll then see his heart for you.

A TASTE OF
INVITATION

Behold, I stand at the door and knock. If anyone hears my voice and opens the door, I will come in to him and eat with him, and he with me.

REVELATION 3:20

Take a minute with this verse. Do you zoom in on the part I do? Once Jesus walks through the door of our lives, the first thing he wants to do is eat. As much as I love food, this promise goes much deeper than our plates. Think about the response when Jesus ate with sinners: "And the Pharisees and the scribes grumbled, saying, 'This man receives sinners and eats with them'" (Luke 15:2). Why would they complain that Jesus ate some bread with sinners? Because it wasn't really the food that bothered them; it was that Jesus received sinners that made the hypocrites boil over. We talk about receiving Jesus into our lives, but the amazing thing is that he's received us into his.

So when he knocks, will we let him in?

We must give permission. We must choose to receive the nourishment physical and spiritual food offers. Maybe this is why Jesus held up the bread and the cup as a representation of him: because food cannot ever be anything more than an invitation. Nourishment is a choice. We choose what we take in carefully. Why? Because what we take in becomes who we are. The bite of a strawberry, lick of some ice cream, or sip of a warm coffee gets taken in, broken down, and becomes a part of us. Could this be the essence of Jesus's knock? For us to be open to who Jesus fully is—not just a good teacher but the sustenance for our soul? That knock is the invitation to receive him, our lifeblood, as we would food and water. In his only recorded prayer for those who believe and will believe in him, this is exactly what he requested of the Father: "That they may all be one, just as you, Father, are in me, and I in you, that they also may be in us" (John 17:20-21). This is at the heart of love itself: that two become one. Jesus knocks to ensure he enters through love, that he might prepare a feast of love as he holds out to us the most important meal we'll ever eat: the bread and the cup, his body and blood broken and poured out for us, that we become eternally nourished. He says, "whoever feeds on me, he also will live because of me . . . Whoever feeds on this bread will live forever" (John 6:57-58). He knocks so we might receive him through his death, so we might have life.

Jesus knocks because of what he wants to give and because of who he is. If he wrote an autobiography, it would be really short, like one sentence kind of short. Jesus said, "I am gentle and lowly in heart" (Matthew 11:29). The Creator of the universe doesn't barge in, because love requires permission; he knocks and waits outside to be invited in. He wants to sit around a table with us. Isn't that the best part of a good meal? To laugh, talk, and partake of not just the nourishment of the food but of the company itself? "Better is a dinner of herbs where love is than a fattened ox and hatred with it" (Proverbs 15:17). Even the most delicious meal is spoiled when there's a lack of love. Assimilating nutrients and digestion are dependent upon the body feeling safe, so Jesus, being meek and lowly, knocks because he loves. He carried the cross so he could one day cross the threshold of our hearts, but love isn't love without permission. Love must be chosen. And so ...

he knocks,

he asks,

he waits.

May our hearts remember the hands that were nailed to the tree, that we might taste and see the goodness of God's love. May we be nourished by his broken body, that he might make us whole. May we receive a nourishment so deep it goes past our bones and makes its way down to our souls. A nourishment so deep that the life it brings us is not just temporary but eternal. May we receive Jesus because he first received us.

NEVER-ENDING
NOURISHMENT

May we open our hearts to his Word every morning, not out of obligation but invitation to let his heart pour into ours.

Jesus said, "Follow me." As we watch what he does, we're invited to do as he did.

May we acknowledge our Father in heaven and invite his will to reach down from above. Let's ask for both our daily bread and forgiveness as we forgive others. Request to be led far from temptation and delivered from the evil one. Seeking first the kingdom because it's his.

Let's be like Jesus—in continual conversation with the Father. Faithful to rest. To get alone in a quiet place. To know the Scriptures. To gather at the house of God to worship him. To walk with other believers and be salt and light to the world.

As the sunrise washes us afresh with mercy from heaven, let's accept the invitation to start a new habit to be with him.

Entering his Word gives us light; let's open it up and let it pour in.

Whether you fill up with one chapter or one verse, for one minute or one hour, time spent with God is fruitful, always.

Let's dive deep into each page to discover the treasures in the Scriptures. As we do, we'll find our own lives being written out by him. We find his Word energizes us for the day and infuses our life with direction.

My hope is we'll remember every morning that our lives count for eternity. Come to Jesus today, tomorrow, and every day. We'll discover fresh mercy, a restored soul, and a renewed heart as we continue to come, taste, and see.

For a more detailed reading plan, head to
cambriajoy.com/milkandhoney
to continue your journey.

MEET
CAMBRIA

I live, write, and create content in a small beach town in California with my husband, Bo, and my little dog, Meester. I love getting lost in a book, going on a sunset walk by the sea, making fresh food, and having a good conversation about Jesus.

I've been a wellness and lifestyle YouTuber since 2010, and at the heart of it all is content to help you dive deep into wellness that changes you from the inside out. This verse encapsulates it well: "Beloved, I pray that all may go well with you and that you may be in good health, as it goes well with your soul" (3 John 1:2). You're in my heart with every video I create, and I hope you feel God's heart toward you as you watch.

My first book, *Growing Strong*, provides practical help, exercises, devotions, and encouragement for the physical and spiritual journey. I hold a certified personal trainer license and nutrition coach certification through the National Academy of Sports Medicine.

You're welcome to watch my videos on YouTube. Just search Cambria Joy, and subscribe to the emails I send out to receive weekly refreshment for your body and soul. Think of our inbox hangouts like getting together for coffee every Wednesday. They're everyone's favorite for a reason!

We can hang out more at cambriajoy.com.

SATISFACTION CAN'T BE FOUND IN THE **MIRROR.**
IT'S ONLY FOUND IN **GOD.**

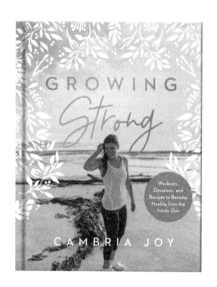

I spent years chasing after a "perfect body" that I believed would make me happy. Instead, I wound up exhausted on the outside and feeling empty on the inside.

What God showed me is that true strength—physical, emotional, and spiritual—grows from the inside out.

Growing Strong includes devotions from God's Word to strengthen your soul, delicious recipes to nourish your body, and creative workouts to keep you moving.

You were not put on this earth to chase after a body that is only temporary.

It's time to turn your eyes away from the mirror and put them back on what truly matters.

Cover design by Faceout Studio, Jeff Miller
Cover photo © Inkling Design (vintage floral frame), dizamax (landscape), Rebellion Works (rays), Mitoria (flourish), Yamurchik (bee) / Shutterstock
Interior design by Nicole Dougherty

For bulk, special sales, or ministry purchases, please call 1-800-547-8979.
Email: Customerservice@hhpbooks.com

 This logo is a federally registered trademark of the Hawkins Children's LLC. Harvest House Publishers, Inc., is the exclusive licensee of this trademark.

Milk and Honey

Copyright © 2024 by Cambria Joy Dam-Mikkelsen
Published by Harvest House Publishers
Eugene, Oregon 97408
www.harvesthousepublishers.com

ISBN 978-0-7369-7808-8 (hardcover)
ISBN 978-0-7369-7809-5 (eBook)

Library of Congress Control Number: 2022948964

Printed in Colombia

23 24 25 26 27 28 29 30 31 / NI / 10 9 8 7 6 5 4 3